M000316004

To: Bi
from — dr Edw
VI
Happy memories!
8 - 16 - 04

MEMORY

from margi — when we went
on trip to n.D. in 2004 with
Ray + margi — Herb + Paula etc
to Sturgess also —

STORIES

By Edward F. Keller, D.D.S.

529 Second Avenue West

Dickinson, North Dakota 58601

August, 1997

MEMORY STORIES

In *"Memory Stories"* author Edward F. Keller demonstrates incredible detailed recollections of his early childhood at his Strasburg, North Dakota farm. In stories like, *My Mother's Apron, Daily Mass, Horse Power* and the many others, Keller evokes the wholesome, sacrificing and hard working spirit of his German Russian ancestors during the 1920's and 1930's in Emmons County, North Dakota. During the past two years these stories have been published weekly in the *Emmons County Record*, Linton, North Dakota.

Copies of this book can be obtained by writing to:

Edward F. Keller, D.D.S.
529 Second Avenue West
Dickinson, ND 58601
Telephone: [701] 225-5302 (home)

$17.50 includes postage and handling

BOOKS BY THE AUTHOR

As I Remember, 1994 . . . unpublished

My First World, 1995 . . . published

Memories Stories, 1997 . . . published

Sheila, 1997 . . . unpublished

My Second World . . . in progress . . . author's formative years

From Kadon to Implants . . . in progress . . . author's 42 years in dentistry

Memory Stories II . . . in progress

Amateur Writer (How I wrote, self published and marketed the first fourteen years of my life) . . . in progress

MEMORY STORIES

by: Edward F. Keller

I wish to thank my wife, Shirley, she patiently critiques all my writing. I also wish to thank Allan Burke, editor of the *Emmons County Record*, for being so good to me the past two years.

Copyright: Edward F. Keller

1997

INDEX

Memory Stories:

Excerpts from *My First World*:

EHLI, THE GUITAR MAN

My 1938 and 1939 seventh and eighth grade teacher at Wells School #18, nine miles east of Linton on Beaver Creek was Ehli Cruschwutz. Ehli hailed from Cooperstown, was married (her name escapes me) and they had a school aged son named Lyle. They lived with John Horners, along with two of Horner's married sons with their children plus Horner's own four single children (which almost qualified them to incorporate as a village).

Ehli was a talented guitarist and balladeer. He held his highly polished light and dark brown instrument with a golden rope shoulder strap, a tassel dangling at the bottom as his strumming hand glided over the strings and his other hand fingered the chords. Ehli was the first man I had ever seen who sang in English and played an instrument other than an accordion and who wore half pants not held up with suspenders. He sounded like the Carter Family from far off Texas on my floor model radio. Ehli sang and played often in school and I was captivated by his music.

I begged my father to use my scrap iron money to purchase a $3.00 guitar from Andy Kraft. It was maroon in color and had no carrying case. I took it to school in a gunny sack. Ehli taught me three positions in the G chord and I learned to play and sing *Cowboy Jack* . . ."He was just a lonely cowboy, with a heart so brave and true. And he learned to love a maiden, with eyes of heavenly blue." And another song in the G chord I learned was *Little Brown Jug* . . . "My wife and I lived all alone in a little brown hut we called our own. She loved gin and I loved rum and that's the way we had lots of fun. Ha, ha, ha, you and me, little brown jug how I love thee. Tis you who makes my friends and foes, tis you who makes me wear old clothes, etc." (My mental computer fails to expel these items along with my 1946 Army serial number, RA 17185919, sir).

Many years later I totally surprised 10 year old son, Joey, with these melodies on a guitar at a music store. He caught the bug, purchased a guitar, took lessons from Kim Bozekowski, appeared in many recitals and competitions, acquired stage presence and confidence, all very complementary to his adult business world in Minneapolis, Minnesota. Thank you Ehli Cruschwutz.

* * * * * *

MY MOTHER'S APRON

A vivid childhood memory is my mother's apron. My mother began her day by donning her cotton bib apron. It made her come alive and ready for mothers' work. Self made on her sewing machine the apron had a heavy neck collar and strong belt strands that tied in the back. One side pocket contained a handkerchief for my nose and hers while the other had raisins or blackjack gum from the Watkins man in case I had good behavior. When mother brought up the hem of this knee length garment there formed an enormous pouch which served as a transport for whatever needed to be.

She carried firewood and dried corn cobs and dried cow chips to the kitchen stove and loaves of baked bread from the oven to the pantry in her apron. On wash day the apron held clothes pins and washed diapers. Eggs from the hen house cradled in her apron pouch. Baby chicks, baby kittens and baby piglets nestled there on their way to the warmth of our house. Once a baby jackrabbit from the field enjoyed an apron ride to become my pet.

From the potato patch her apron bore new fresh potatoes. The garden yielded green onions, fresh carrots, radishes and pickling cucumbers to mother's apron. From the melon patch the apron brought cantaloupe and honeydews. The dough pan rested in the apron on her lap (as I hung on her knees and ate the peelings). Pumpkins being grated with a spoon for blachinda found support in her aproned lap. The baby enjoyed motherly warmth and sweet smelling powder in her apron after a bath.

When my mother unwrapped herself from her work-stained apron it was the end of the day. The only time she didn't wear her apron was when visiting, going to town or on church days.   * * * * *

DAILY MASS

My mother and father retired to Linton in 1945 at ages 45 and 55 respectively. Years of farming by hand and horses, minus electricity and indoor plumbing had extracted volumes of strength and imposed aches and bruises beyond their years. They had known only work, four kinds: spring work, summer work, fall work and winter work, all interspersed with regular work and blizzards of snow and dust, drought and grasshoppers.

In town, church replaced morning chores. Visiting the first winter, I woke one morning to groaning floor boards and running sinks at 5:30 a.m. Mother nudged my door with, "Coming to 6 o'clock Mass?" A peek at the early dawn had lights popping on all around the neighborhood. My folks lived just east of St. Anthony's Church, in the corner house. We left the house and the frosted air whitened our breath as it did the exhaust of church going cars. Mother's gray woolen shawl and long black coat blended into the throng of silhouettes converging on the church. There were the Richters, the Schmaltzes, the Wagners, the Fettigs, the Vetters, the Bosches all reaching the railings up the multi, multi steps to the entrance. I left mother on the womens' side and joined the men.

A tingling in the sacristy announced the priest and the server boys approaching the altar to begin their quiet exchange of Latin prayers. Some of the faithful took black, gold edged missals with yellow silk bookmark stringers hanging from them. Most reached for rosaries, unraveled them with seasoned hands, kissed the little crucifix, made the sign of the cross and left it dangling from the side of the pew---their lips moving in silent Creeds, Our Fathers, Hail Marys and Glory Bes. Prayers perhaps for atonement, perhaps thanksgiving for retirement bounty, perhaps a request for help to a son taking up wine or a daughter cigarettes, or perhaps just a store of prayers to assure the heavenly goal. At Holy Communion time there were few takers. These people deemed themselves unworthy to receive Christ but a couple times a year.

My father attended the 8 a.m. Mass, the one where school children marched to the pews as the good, holy hooded sisters demanded reverence and tugged the undisciplined. They sang and prayed and my father fingered his large wooden, brown, marble sized beads with three inch crucifix, the one from Russia yet, that once was his mother's. He enjoyed the young people and the later hour.

* * * * *

MY FIRST GRADE AND SCHOOLMATES, 1932

At Emmons County Wells School #18 near my Rosenthal church, Miss Wells, the slender, dark, pretty teacher with a spit curl crossing her forehead, says I can start school at age five because I have Frank, Debert, Wilma and Mary to watch for me. We drive the three miles in a sled or buggy with Dave and Tootsy. As we pass through Hagel's farm we pick up their cousin, Martha Vetsch, a pretty girl with a light face and light hair, who lives with them. Martha's home is in Burnstad and why she lives with them I don't know. They treat her real nice. When we were almost to school we pass through Klein's farm and Maggie, Rose and Joe Klein join our ride. Klein's mother is my godmother and pays attention to me and encourages Tootsy and Dave and I feel happy. At school the team has its very own stall in the red barn and eats the hay we sat on.

Joe, John, Helen and Frank Kuhn also come with a team smaller and faster than Tootsy and Dave. Tony Kelsch rides his pony, Spike. Jake, Joe and Mary Horner walk their mile unless the weather is too cold, then their older brother, Peter, takes them in a sled. Joe Vetter walks his half a mile to school. To get warm before classes I gather with all the students around the red hot stove. The smell of coal, varnish and earlier barn chores permeate the room.

Singing is the first of the 15 minute class sessions. *My Country Tis of Thee, Old Black Joe, Old MacDonald* and *Carry Me Back To Old Virginie* fill the room. The bigger boys , Joe Kuhn, Jake Horner and brother, Frank, seem to be singing a different way with their low voices. Class sessions at the front of the room are recitals and teacher talking. During eighth grade Agriculture I hear about Leghorns, Plymouth

Rocks, Guernseys, Holsteins, Percherons and Belgians. Fifth grade Geography is about Bismarck, North Dakota, Pierre, South Dakota and Sacramento, California. I and my first graders, Joe Vetter, Joe Klein and Frank Kuhn say the alphabet and learn words in English. Then its time for a 15 minute recess and a fox and goose game in the snow. More class and then lunch hour follows.

Everyone eats at their desks. Miss Wells has lettuce sandwiches and drinks from a black thermos. Martha has a blue lunch box and thermos with orange or red nectar. She shares bites of her jelly bread and pieces of chicken with me---a welcome complement to my syrup sandwiches from a gallon syrup pail. Tony Kelsch enjoys hard boiled eggs and syrup sandwiches. The Kuhn children have cream with sprinkled sugar sandwiches. Joe Vetter loves sausage from the night before with plain bread. The Horners too have syrup sandwiches. I watch Mary Horner eat. She is the prettiest one in the school. During lunch hour I play at Beaver Creek, skate on the ice, watch bunnies, pheasants, climb trees and slide down snow banks. I wish I could live on Beaver Creek like the Kleins, Kelsches and the Horners.

After lunch hour are more front of the room classes. My sister, Mary, and Helen Kuhn recite poems. I'm afraid Mary may get stuck and I almost start to cry. Joe Horner spells Chicago and Miss Wells pats him on the shoulder. Next there is the last recess period for games and fresh air and then the final class sessions. I go to the blackboard to write 1, 2, 3, 4 and get all the way to 12. Miss Wells pats my shoulder and I sit down.

At the end of the day I gather my four cent tablet and penny pencil and school things. Tootsy and Dave love to run home. I can't wait to tell about the day to my mother and father.   * * * * *

TRIX, BESSIE, PENNY AND LADY

During "My First World" Valentine Kelsch lived northeast of Rosenthal Church, following Highway #13 towards the St. Michael's area. I could not find the farm today because as a little boy I only knew the seven square miles west and south of Rosenthal, between Linton and Strasburg.

The sound of Valentine Kelsch's name invoked happy feelings along with the Fourth of July and Christmas. That farm raised shetland ponies, many of them, 50 - 60 at a time. I often begged my father to take me to the pony farm. My body would shake with excitement as we approached the farm. The ponies would be in little groups as Valentine corralled them for us. There were stallions, mothers with colts, pintos of all colors, some all black with white faces, some all white and all brown with white socks. Their little heads were so cute and their little hooves formed such cute snow and dirt tracks. The little bridles with short reins had tiny bits for their tiny mouths. They smelled good and had fine hair. They were easy to mount and had short stubby gaits. I needed to be balanced and alert to their swift change of direction. Suddenly the whole world was my size. Along with my parents, godmother, school and church, shetland ponies were my love.

I had a big pony, Bessie, that doubled as a working horse. My father found it difficult to justify an extra mouth to feed just as a pet. He finally gave in when Anton

Ibach, who lived near Ibach Lake, near Stopplers south and east of Rosenthal, had an extra shetland pony. My father traded a calf and a sack of left over seed wheat for Trix. I loved Trix and so did my father who was so happy for me. I rode and played with him everyday.

Many years later, living in Dickinson with children of my own, I bought Penny, a pinto shetland pony, and also Lady, a big white pony. We dug a well on ten acres, built a little barn and played farm. We horsebacked into the country and rode in parades. Penny and Lady towed toboggans and sleds full of kids with ropes tied to their saddles. That was all so much fun for us, thanks to Valentine Kelsch, Anton Ibach and my father.

* * * * *

HORSEPOWER

Harry died a willing worker. Frank Jangula was hauling wheat to Linton from our farm in the spring of 1939 when his truck got stuck in a muddy road ditch. My brother, Debert, harnessed up Harry, the big stallion, and hitched him to the front of the truck to help gain forward motion. Harry sensed the challenge, leaped forward, broke the harness straps and ran off screaming in agony. He shortly laid down and died, no doubt with a ruptured vital organ. We were very deeply saddened by the loss of Harry.

Five years previous we had bred Harry's mother to a purebred stallion on the James farm north of Highway #13 about four miles from Linton. Harry had a big muscular build and weighed nearly a ton. He had a reddish brown color with a black mane and tail. His disposition was gentle. I used him as a pony to fetch the mail and gather the cows from the pasture. Riding Harry was like driving a locomotive. His broad body forced my legs apart as I barebacked him. We also used Harry as a team horse. His best partner was a gelding named Tarzan, his full brother. They were friends and worked well together hauling hay to the barn, manure from the barn, cultivating corn and mowing hay.

Stallions were kept in the barn year round because they could be cruel to geldings or jump a fence to romance neighboring mares. Horses were bred only during the months of May or June so that colts could be born in the spring of the year. A winter colt had rough sledding in below zero weather.

Neighboring farmers bred their mares at our farm. They sought nice looking colts and wanted Harry to be the father. We charged a fee of $6.00 after a colt was born.

In the 1930's farmers maintained fifteen to eighteen horses to work their farms. A horse needed to be two or three years old before it was broke for work. It took five horses to pull a two-bottom plow and four to pull a seed drill. During harvest six horses drove a header plus two for the header box that gathered the shocks. Horses were well cared for. During the winter months they were fed, watered and groomed and kept in the barn nights. It was a must that they be ready for spring plantings and summer harvest.   * * * * *

SCHMALTZ MEATS

In "My First World" time, when I was a little boy, a most intriguing visitor to my farm was the butcher, in the person of John Schmaltz Sr. or one of his sons, John Jr., Tony, Ralph or Adam. When he arrived in his pickup I rode with him to identify the cow my father said he could butcher.

9

As we encircled the herd, bouncing through the prairie, the cows grew frisky. They stood shoulder to shoulder, droolings dangling from the corners of their rubbery lips. After the shotgun, Mr. Schmaltz drove close and unloaded a scaffolding, rope, tackle and pulley to hoist and hang the cow by the hind legs. With keen edged knives he quickly skinned the animal (like I did jackrabbits), severed the head and feet, and placed the hide on the pickup. After slicing the length of the midsection he dressed out all but the liver, heart and tongue. These he placed into a pail of water on the truck. Then he rinsed the carcass from a barrel on his truck and sawed it vertically in half. Next he pulled the halves into his vehicle, dismantled and loaded the scaffolding, leaving the remains to the coyotes, crows and vultures. Mr. Schmaltz dropped me off back at the farm house and drove to the butcher shop in Strasburg. There he cut the meat into steaks, roasts, borscht soup meat and sausage meat. Schmaltz's ring bologna recipe, smoked, boiled and ready to eat cold, appeared on everybody's menu.

I loved visiting Schmaltz's Butcher Shop and Grocery. The full cookie jars, candy shelves, 10 pound bulks of halvah, fruit and vegetable window displays so impressed me. Mother handed the clerk a grocery list. He gathered the items into a paper box and carried it to the car. Sometimes I lunched in the back room, sitting on apple boxes and eating store bread, ring bologna and watermelon. Mr. Schmaltz served delicious cider (fruit extract) from a wooden barrel in his cooler.

John Schmaltz Sr. immigrated from Russia in 1892 at the age of twelve. His family settled in St. Anthony. There he grew up and married Clara Bullinger. In 1910 Clara and John and several small children came across the river and founded Schmaltz

Meats at Strasburg. Mr. Schmaltz, or "Das Schmeltzle" as he was lovingly referred to, exuded friendly warmth that permeated the store. In his full length apron he smiled at patrons and managed the store with the help of his children, Margaret, Adam, John Jr., Tony, Ralph, Mary, Martina, Rose, Agatha, Agnes, Frances, Mike, Leo, Hugo, Clara and Felicia. In 1936 Schmaltz Meats moved to Linton and operated much the same. John Schmaltz Sr. died in 1951. Schmaltz Meats and the famous ring bologna recipe passed on to John Jr., then to grandson Melvin Schmaltz and in 1997, after 87 years, to great grandson, Brian Schmaltz.

* * * * *

FENCES

In "My First World" time, miles of fences encompassed my prairie farm empire, an empire built to last, to be handed down to grandchildren to grow up on and farm in their turn. Fences in such perfect lines they might have been drawn on the land with a ruler and a pencil, divided my veldt. They trailed mile square section lines as they dipped into valleys and ascended hills into the horizon. Fences were often shared by two neighbors. At times each neighbor built his own, four feet apart, as was the case with mine, Wolfs, Hagels and Kelsches. Internal fences kept cattle from wheat fields, hogs from gardens and milk cows in the milk fence.

Fences tamed the land long before schoolhouses and churches. Each farm had five to seven miles of fence, 500 posts per mile, with two or three double stranded barbed wires, drawn violin string tight with a block and pulley. Corners and gates demanded extra skill and ingenuity. Fences were more tedious to build than houses and barns.

Posts harvested from Beaver Creek, rickety, crooked and thin, needed frequent replacement. River bottom posts, wedged and split from larger trees, were more durable and metal posts most desirable and expensive. Fences made statements about their builders and farmers took pride in their work.

In addition to declaring a domain and containing livestock, some fences carried talk-a-phone wire, stretched on the posts to connect mile apart farms. Phone boxes on kitchen walls with their dring, dring, dring---one and a half for Wolfs, two for Kleins, two and a half for Krafts and three for Schwabs, broke the prairie loneliness as did the train whistles. No privacy prevailed, but any conversation with other people was reviving.

* * * * *

MINNESOTA VACATION

August 10th through 17th Shirley and I, our four Twin City sons and their families plus Tom's mother-in-law, Joan, met at Sandy Beach Resort on one of Minnesota's 10,000 inland water bodies, Gull Lake. Sandy Beach was just that. Kindly sand extended from shallow clear water to the picnic furniture filled lawn. Mammoth oaks overhung the cabins which contained ample bedrooms, kitchens, living rooms and baths for comfortable living. Squirrels, chipmunks, ducks and gulls scrambled for blueberries, Cheerios and bread chunks as their child friends fed them. A game room and playground, steps away, presented a childrens' (there were seven under six) haven. I particularly enjoyed the morning kiddie parades of bikes and strollers on the paved roadways enclosed by trees and flowers filled with serenading birds, even a deer and a mail box with "Keller" on it.

The Pines, Minnesota's #1 ranked public 18 holes was unrelentless and less suited for hackers (but fair) than the West 18 at Madden's Resort. Shops and mini golf and water slides at nearby Nisswa and Pequot Lakes satisfied tastes of some of us eighteen. John's boat provided soothing rides along the 30 mile shoreline, docking at eateries for burgers, foot longs and fries---and yes, meeting the Minnesota loon.

Family conversation, lawn picnics, close living, grandchildren hugs, breakfast coffee somehow made the tough love of 25 years past all worth while and made me more like a reaper than the sower in time gone by. I'd do it again.

* * * * *

BRAUCHE

With her bare left foot gently resting on my abdomen, as I was lying on the floor, she read from a piece of paper, handed down by her mother, Schlag aus dieses kindes ribben, Jesus lag in der kripe. Vater, Sohn, Heiliger Geist. (Depart from this child's ribs, Jesus lay in the crib. Father, Son, Holy Ghost). Mother repeated these words three times and gave me warm camomile tea to drink. I picked camomile blossoms from a ditch wild patch by the clothesline. Looking up into her face I saw a determined, faith possessing expression absolutely absorbed in the healing power of God. This particular faith-ritual cured "angewachsen" (adhesions) anywhere on my body trunk, caused by bruises, falls or too many chokecherry or watermelon seeds. I always recovered.

A sty found my mother blowing into the affected eye while reading from her guarded piece of paper. "Schussblotter geh raus, oder ich rab dich mit mein rechten

13

daume raus. Vater, Sohn, Heiliger Geist. (Sty blister go away, or I'll rub you out with my right thumb. Father, Son, Holy Ghost). Repeated three times.

Mother transferred warts from my body to a piece of string or a dishcloth and buried them in a misthaufe (manure pile).

Her healing arsenal contained not just faith and magic. She applied liniment, camphor salve, camomile tea, laying on of hands and feet, and message, all depending on the diagnosis.

My father did Brauche for the horses. Their lame legs, shoulder collar sores and fence cuts all received laying on of hands, massages, prayer rituals, salves, string transfers and liniment. "Tell me those words again," he'd say as mother fetched the sacred piece of paper and read to him till he memorized the prayers. For horses liniment mixed into water was substituted for camomile tea. There was a gurgling noise as it swished down their long throats from a quart sized beer bottle.

* * * * *

LETTER TO DAVID JOHN KELLER

February 2nd, 1997

Dearest David John:

Your father called your grandmother, Shirley, and me this morning to announce your birth. Welcome, David, to the greatest country on earth. Since the United States of America was born on July 4th, 1776, people the world wide have rushed to live here. The person responsible for us Kellers living here, David, is Phillip Keller, your great-great-great grandfather.

Phillip's father once lived in the German-speaking French province of Alsace, about 194 years ago. When warlike rulers like Napoleon abused him there he migrated to Odessa, Russia on the Black Sea, where the Czar Alexander welcomed him with free land, freedom from conscription, free school and freedom to worship as he pleased.

Phillip was born in Russia in about 1835, grew up there, married and raised eight children: Mike, your great-great-grandfather, Johannnas, Joseph, Sebastian, Valentine, Margaret, Magdelina and Johanna. But soon the Czar became jealous of how well these hard working Germans were doing in Russia. He denied them conscription freedoms, religious worship and schools. Wars developed. Stalin was inventing communism to overthrow the Czar. In the late 1800's America invited Russian people to come and settle Dakota Territory. They offered them free land, religious freedom and to live in a democracy. Phillip purchased a round trip ticket to scout this new land for his children. He went by rail to Hamburg, Germany, by ship to New York, by rail to Aberdeen, South Dakota and by ox cart to Strasburg, North Dakota.

Upon Phillip's return he arranged for his children, ages 30-45 and their own families, to come to America in 1905, and to homestead in Strasburg. Phillip, in his 70's stayed in Russia, an enormous sacrifice, David, because he loved his children and wanted them to live in a free country.

In 1905, Mike, 45, had six children: Franz, 15, (your great-grandfather), Matt, Magdelina, Julia, Amelia and Peter.

Franz married Helen Schneider in 1917 and raised seven children: Frank, Debert, Wilma, Mary, Edward (me, your grandfather), Wilfred and Eleanor.

In 1955, David, I married your grandmother, Shirley Maloney and we were blessed with seven children, Edward Jr., Ann, John (your father), Mary, Tom, Joe and Paul.

Your father married Laurie Abraham in 1988 and besides yourself they have Megan, Ben and Brian.

David, in America you have the freedom to become anything you desire. You can become president.   * * * * *

WHY I WRITE

During the spring of 1938 on our Strasburg farm we had two extra horses. Of the eleven horses we had, four were needed to pull the seed drill and five to pull the two bottom gang plow. These two teams were operated by my two older brothers. To utilize all our horse power my father activated an old one bottom, two horse, walking plow. With the reins over his shoulder and his hands on the guiding handles my father walked many miles in the fresh furrows that spring. I was eleven years old and loved walking along with him in those furrows, talking to him about everything I could think of. One day I told him that I had heard that 1938 was going to be a good crop year (there had been four consecutive no-crop years). His answer was, "Eddie, some day you will become somebody." I have never forgotten the exact spot in the 40 acre field behind the barn, where my father lovingly said these words. This little story, so full of positives, needs to be told. It had and still has great worth.

All adults have a "first world" in which parents, siblings, grandparents, teachers, priests, ministers, governors, presidents, neighbors, aunts, uncles, godparents and other adults said or performed significant memorable print worthy things. Church and school are fertile memory territory. Social and neighborhood happenings contain rich experiences to tell future generations. To put some of these on paper is to leave a worth while legacy.

I write to satisfy a craving for a need to tell someone of my experiences. They helped me grow and could help future children. Writing also serves me as a catharsis, a purging of emotions through art. Writing is the art of creating a story. Paper is patient. Someone will enjoy and benefit from the effort.

* * * * *

MY LAND

My immediate domain, where I played and trapped gophers when I was a little boy in "My First World" time encompassed my land. "You can go anywhere you want to, as long as you stay on our own land," mother commanded.

Places were significant and had names; Badger Hill, Sand Hill, Gopher Hill, Indian Rocks, Jumper Cactus Patch, Juneberry Patch, Gully Waterhole, the Potato Patch, Chokecherry Rock Pile and more. My favorite place was the huge boulder jutting towards the sky on the rimrock hill that curtained my farm. This was my Cathedral, the perch from where I surveyed my land and possessions. Its magnitude and massive tonnage, with a protruding shelf provided shelter from the wind, sun, rain and hail. From the top of it I took pleasure in 360 degrees of blue sky touching earth. Bug-sized cars crawled on the horizon on Highway #13 five miles beyond, halfway to Linton. There was the rooftop of Wolf's barn. In the distant pasture were four side by side hills resembling loaves of bread. One belonged to the Bosches, one to the Wolfs and two were mine. I spied on my cows grazing two miles away.

The sixty acre, twenty acre and nineteen hilly acre fields, 1 1/2 miles away, the ones we bought from Uncle Matt, were in distant view. The forty acre, fifty acre and seven acre fields, once part of Grandpa's homestead, presented a closer view. Fields altered yearly as they changed from corn to wheat to oats or barley.

My perch revealed the farm buildings below, the imposing barn roof sprawling with lean-to sheds, the top of the house with lightning rods, chimney and dormers. I felt a dominating sensation of towering the sky scraper windmill. I enjoyed the reflection of blue sky on the dam just beneath me and the dam narrowing and disappearing in the dry gully to Kraft's land. It was a rich feeling to see my property; wagons, hay racks, sleds, plows, cultivators, mowers, seed drills and the header by my farm. Hay stacks with tire and wire covers seemed less tall.

As I reclined on the flatness of my Cathedral, I could almost touch the fleecy white clouds that formed galloping horses, grazing cows, sheep, cars, faces, churches and Jesus, some holding the shapes for a long time. Then I'd hear a gopher trap snap and the squeal, and another tail worth a penny at the county agent's office.

* * * * *

DEAREST ADRIANNA KATHLEEN:

A phone call from your Minneapolis father Thursday morning, June 9th, 1997, brought the happy news of your birth to your grandmother, Shirley, and me. We welcome you, love you and are anxious to see you soon.

Now is surely a good time for a girl to be born in the United States. Opportunity abounds for girls in our country. Years back girls were never encouraged to become anything else but teachers, nurses, mothers and housewives. In my four years of dental school I knew of only two girls studying to be dentists. They were both Catholic nuns who rejoined their huge convents to do the dental work there. The dental school class of 86, starting this September at the University of Minnesota contains 39 girls. Today girls have equal opportunity with boys in sports, politics, military, dentistry, medicine, law, engineering and in many religious ministries.

The means of formal education in store for you, Adrianna, with all the electronic inventions, are revolutionary. Communication technology and airplanes have shrunk planet earth to a single marketing state. Your work station area may be global, under the ocean or interplanetary and your job not yet invented.

I will be cheering you on, Adrianna, if not from North Dakota from somewhere yet to be decided.

Love,

Grandpa Keller

* * * * *

EWIGKEIT

In" My First World" time, I served Mass at my Sacred Heart country church, eight miles east of Linton. Sacred Heart was a mission of another country church to the east, St. Aloysious, commonly known as, "The Creek". During the winter, Frank Vetter, who lived by my church, had the job of stoking the church furnace hours before

19

services. But on this frigid 35 degree below zero January Sunday morning in 1938, the church's heating system lacked considerable efficiency.

I met pastor, Father Charles Meyer, numbish cold and shivering in the sacristy as he vested with the icy Mass robes. "This church takes an ewigkeit (eternity) to warm up," he mumbled behind his frosty white breath. "How long is ewigkeit?" my eleven-year-old curiosity queried. "Let me tell you Eddie, how long ewigkeit is," he volunteered, as he gazed into the floor length mirror, still adjusting his vestments. "Imagine a huge fifty mile long mountain range, every million years a bird carries one grain of soil from the first mountain of the range to a place twenty miles away. After the first mountain is completely gone a bird will start on the next and so on until the entire mountain range is gone. That is ewigkeit, Eddie."

* * * * *

SUNDAYS

Sundays on my Emmons County farm near Strasburg in the 1920's and 1930's came as a welcome festive day of rest from whatever work was in season, plowing, seeding, haying, harvesting, rock hauling or fencing. Only the milking and chores happened on Sundays. A mood of celebration and experiencing other people after the week's prairie isolation, elevated my spirits.

Saturday's preparation for Sunday included house cleaning. Linoleum patterns reappeared on the floors and clean windows, chairs and tables brightened the house. Summer Saturday bathings in the dam and winter feet and head washing (mother's fingernails and soap in my eyes) all made me feel new.

Occasional winter Saturday baths in a wash tub, two waters, one for the girls and one for the boys, were more difficult. The weekly change of underclothes and socks was a Sunday ritual. My father's weekly shave came right before the Saturday visit to town that stocked the pantry with the cream check money.

For church I dressed in a suit, white shirt, tie and Sunday shoes, in the nicest room in the house, the "shtup," where the Sunday clothes hung in a "shonk", a free standing closet, as the "Little Bohemian Band" played a Sunday morning radio show from a station in Dickinson. Bohemian music featured lead horns, while Strasburg German music had accordion leads. Mother made me brush my teeth and use hair oil, "That's enough, just a little on your hands and rub it into your hair."

On the drive to 9 o'clock Low Mass or 10:30 High Mass I sat in the rear seat of our 1927 Chevrolet with my parents and little siblings. In the front seat my oldest brother drove the car, my older sister sat next to him and the second oldest brother was on the door side, to open the gates. On the pasture trail to the section line road, unwelcome parental driving advice, "Careful, that rock will soon hit high center between the ruts," and "Keep the speed going so you can make the hill," surfaced from the back seat.

Before and after church, parishioners visited in bunches, according to age and gender. Either mother or an older girl in my family would stay home from church to oversee the special Sunday meal, "Add the carrots in twenty minutes and the cabbage in thirty minutes, etc., to the borscht soup." The festive Sunday meals alternated from borscht to chicken soup. Borscht produced the stringy square of boiled beef to which was

21

added catsup sauce gravy for the mashed potatoes. Chicken soup left boiled chicken for the catsup gravy. Graham cracker crust lemon meringue or apple pie finished off the Sunday dinner.

On Sunday afternoons my parents stayed dressed in Sunday clothes and visited neighbors and friends or neighbors and friends came to our house. I joined them and my playmates at the Kleins, Krafts, Baumans, Hagels and others. Older brothers and sisters visited their age groups at farms. Sometimes Matt and Pete Schwab, John Hagel or Tony Bauman brought accordions for instant entertainment. Adults stayed for supper and ring bologna, potato salad, chocolate cake and red jello with bananas featured the favorite menu.

At times when there was no company or visiting mother made ice cream for supper. Sunday evenings brought the "Jack Benny Show" on the radio, with Mary Livingston, Phil Harris and Rochester during the supper hour. I was saddened with the passing of Sunday.   * * * * *

FIRST CHRISTMAS AWAY

In 1941, at age 14, I spent my first Christmas away from home at the Precious Blood Seminary boarding school. Brunnerdale Seminary in Canton, Ohio operated the first three years of high school, St. Joseph's Academy and College in Rensselaer, Indiana the last year of high school and first two years of college. St. Charles Seminary, Carthagena, Ohio furnished the last six years of seminary study. Today Brunnerdale is the Glenmoore Country Club, St. Charles a retirement home for priests and St. Joseph's

22

a flourishing co-ed college. Father Charles Meyer, our pastor at Rosenthal in 1941 who took me to Ohio is in his nineties and a resident at St. Charles.

The Christmas tradition at Brunnerdale, as I found out after Christmas, entailed all the priests, nuns, brothers, second and third year students surprising the first year students with the most joyful Christmas possible. This year 1941 especially needed to have some joy because World War II had just been declared and many of us had loved ones in the armed forces (my brother, Frank, at Camp Claiborne, Louisiana with the American Infantry Division later fought three year in the South Pacific).

Father Neumeyer, sacristan and in charge of Christmas decorations constructed a manger and crib scene covering half of the foyer leading to the chapel. The near life sized figurines tending baby Jesus in the crib were surrounded by animals in the manger whose walls were pine branches and cones, all under a deep blue star filled sky with the brightest star shining on Jesus. Red, blue and green bulbs in the pine illuminated the pleasingly dim scene. The smell of pine permeated the cheerful, tearful, celestial, serene atmosphere in the foyer. It was so inviting to kneel and pray by. I just wanted to be near it and gaze at it and I actually was glad I wasn't home.

On Christmas morning the first year class was awakened with "*Silent Night*" by the third year octet instead of the usual cowbell. After Low Mass and morning prayers the Great Silence which began with night prayers and usually ended after breakfast was lifted before breakfast. The Sisters had decorations all over the priest's, brothers' and students' tables. There were oranges, bananas, apples, juices, sweet rolls and other breakfast food, absolutely the most elaborate breakfast setting I had ever seen. With the octet caroling and students talking in festive spirit, Santa Claus, in the person of Brother Tony, made his entrance carrying a large red sack full of candy and nuts. I recognized Tony on account of his crippled left hand. Three months previous during our annual potato dig he, our farm boss, accidently got his hand between two caterpillar lugs that squeezed off four fingers. Brother Tony was kind, patient and encouraging to us. He added to my joy. After breakfast, mail and packages from home were distributed. Then it was time for High Mass, featuring the boys choir and all the lovely readings which I had all but memorized. The Christmas dinner followed. The afternoon was taken with visiting by parents of boys who lived within reasonable distance---entire families would come. They made it a point to include me and boys from Kansas and South Dakota. That night during the Great Silence I meditated the wonderful Christmas I had and looked forward to making next years' first year students happy. (The seminary never used terms freshmen or seniors, only first and fourth, so that we never thought we were ever finished until we reached twelfth. There was never a graduation ceremony until the very end.)   * * * * *

A LETTER FROM MIKE

Dear Edward F. Keller, D.D.S.

After reading your last article, I can't help but drop you a short note. Hope you have time to read this. I am Mike Voller, born and raised 2 1/2 miles east of Strasburg. About 4 - 5 miles southeast of Debert Keller's farm where I understand you were born and raised. I am about your age, so I can relate to all that you write about; the farms, neighbors, town and church. Though we didn't belong to a country mission church, our closest church was Saints Peter & Paul Catholic Church at Strasburg. I, too, was in World War II but I was Navy Amphibious. I served almost two years on the U.S.-L.S.T.-876. I just suppose you know what an L.S.T. is. We were in the Pacific Theater-from Pearl Harbor to Okinawa and every Island between.

Speaking of when and where we were born and raised? At that time five miles was a long way off. Linton was 10 - 13 miles from our farm and I didn't get there until I was in high school. Bismarck was something you heard of, but I only got there when I was bout 20 years of age, shortly before I left for the Navy at Minneapolis, Minnesota. Unheard of before.

I enjoy your articles---keep them coming. Those people our age who grew up on the farms or small towns can relate to those "Good old days."

Happy Holidays and the best in '97 and after.

Sincerely,

Mike

P.S. I know, Debert, your brother real well.

Dear Mike,

Thank you for the thoughtful letter. It makes me happy to know you enjoy the columns and that we are brothers in time. Travel sure wasn't one of our hobbies in the 1930's. I only knew the people who lived on the road to Strasburg, Linton, school and church from our farm. I remember my parents talking about "da Faeler Doony"---Tony Voller, your father I'd guess.

Yes, Mike, I know the U.S.-L.S.T.-876 was a landing ship tank carrier that supplied tanks in the South Pacific, not a fun place to be in World War II. You guys were all heros. I was stationed at an Orthopedic Army hospital with the dental department in Battle Creek, Michigan. Percy Jones was the name of it. We received the casualties from Okinawa. I was astounded at the facial wounds. The doctors grafted ribs into shot off jaw bones and constructed dentures on them. Our dental laboratory also made plastic eyes and skull plates in the reconstruction process. I was a nineteen year old technician half in shock sometimes. Although he wasn't from Okinawa, Bob Dole was one of our patients. He happened to marry one of the nurses.

Mike, you talk about miles and distances in the 1930's. We had a large family of cousins living in Strasburg who had very little to eat. Many a Sunday five or six of these little children walked the six miles to our farm for a borscht and beef and pie dinner and stayed for a fresh spring chicken supper. You remember, Mike, a fresh springer was one who cackled at four o'clock and by six o'clock rested in steaming catsup cream sauce near a sliced loaf of dunking bread and a platter of mashed potatoes. My father often drove the children back to town after supper.

Well, Mike, thanks again for writing and for giving me this chance to talk with you.

Sincerely,

Ed Keller

* * * * *

26

MY FIRST TRAIN RIDE

My first train ride covered from Canton, Ohio to Chicago, Illinois the summer of 1942. I was on a Pennsylvania Railroad train on my way home to Strasburg after my first year of seminary high school in Canton, Ohio. I was overtaken by the elegance and comfort as it swayed through Ohio, Indiana and Illinois to Chicago Union Station. All trains came to and left from Chicago's Union Station.

World War II was on and troops were moving. At Union Station platoons of soldiers and sailors marched by commands to their proper departing gates. I scurried about half a mile to the Milwaukee Road gate, following the directions Father Wagner had given me before he said goodbye, sat and watched in bewilderment all the people and goings on. Union Station was by far the largest building I had ever seen---ever imagined. I boarded the Olympian train for Milwaukee, St. Paul, Ortonville, Aberdeen and Roscoe, South Dakota. The Milwaukee branch led from Roscoe to Artas, South Dakota. The line ended in Linton.

The Milwaukee Road had long been established as a wonderful service before 1942 and in its early years was know as the Chicago, Milwaukee and St. Paul Railroad. As early as 1912 it serviced three Olympian trains in a 24 hour period on a 72 hour trip from Tacoma, Washington to Chicago, Illinois. The Olympian train sported the comforts of sleeping cars, dining cars, compartment cars, parlor and lounge cars and scenic cars; class travel. By 1934 travel time was drastically reduced as the train gained speeds of 112 miles per hour. (Today's Amtrack speed is 80 miles per hour.) In 1947 the Olympian Hiawatha train was established and the Milwaukee Road prided itself with a luxurious train service as it passed through the cities of Tacoma, Missoula, Miles City, Harlowton, Hettinger, Roscoe, Aberdeen, Ortonville, St. Paul, Milwaukee and Chicago.

Linton not only had the round house for the Milwaukee branch, it also had the round house for a Northern Pacific branch line heading to Temvik, Hazelton, McKenzie and Bismarck. Traveling eastward for school and the military, I often road the Milwaukee branch to Roscoe, South Dakota. I enjoyed the whistle as it told the farmers the time of day. There was a lone coach among the freight and cream can cars. Soot from the engine smoke penetrated the windows and doors of the coach. Every seat, window sill, wall and floor of the coach was covered with soot. The palms of my hands were black and all my clothes were freckled with the black stuff. All the air smelled of charcoal. I remember an occasional passenger peeling an orange and changing the scent. The train stopped everywhere it seemed, sometimes in the open prairie, to let an oncoming train pass, or just to check a rattling axle. The trip to Roscoe took four to five hours. The depot there had a worn wooden floor, a pot bellied stove and the smell of varnish. Trainmen perched behind cages, sold tickets for the Olympian Hiawatha on the main line, eastbound for bigger civilization.

* * * * *

RELIGION IN THE 1930'S

Like the rest of the children in the 1930's I learned religion from two sources, church and home. I never missed a Sunday, Holy Day, wedding or funeral at Rosenthal Church in Emmons County, North Dakota. There was catechism before Mass and during a two week summer school session taught by Ignatz Huhn in German. Confession on

Saturday afternoon or before Sunday Mass happened about twice a year. The belief was that nobody but a priest was worthy of receiving Christ any more often. I never went to communion without having gone to confession first. As a child I didn't always feel too comfortable telling my sins to a priest. I always knew when I had sins and all sins were serious. My mother did not believe in venial sins. To her sins were all "tod sins" (German for death or mortal sins) and if you died with one of them on your soul there was nothing but hell for you. I had never heard the word "venial" until I went to the seminary high school. But there they had mortal sins of their own, like staring at a friend's sister on visiting Sunday. As a child my biggest confession problem came when the priest asked, "How many times?" He always demanded restitution and I could live with ten Hail Marys or even a rosary. But for stealing he demanded returning the goods. That was much of the impossible because I had already eaten the goods, like, candy from Petrie's Store, watermelon from Hagel's patch or soda crackers from the pantry. Communion required fasting from midnight on and no more new sins since confession. It was a very serious ritual. Some people brought water to church and went immediately to their cars after church to wash down the Body of Christ.

In our home there was a good supply of holy water, palms, crucifixes and large holy pictures on the walls of every room in the house. We stood for prayers before and after every meal. Night prayers had the entire family standing and facing the picture of the last supper in the kitchen-eating-living room and reciting the Our Father, Hail Mary, Apostle's Creed, Act of Contrition, The Seven Sacraments, The Ten Commandments, an Our Father and a Hail Mary to finish. During Lent the rosary took the place of these night prayers. Then we knelt by a chair and a candle was burning on the kitchen table.

If ever my older siblings would go to a dance evenings we would all say night prayers

before they left the house. During these prayer times I felt our house taking on a serene

church atmosphere and I felt comfortable and protected because I was absolutely certain

God was in our midst. One of the rare times my mother gave me nickels was when I

memorized the Ten Commandments, the Act of Contrition and the Confiteor, a long Latin

prayer altar boys had to say at the foot of the altar in the beginning of Mass.

Sundays were special. After church mother and dad kept on their Sunday clothes.

Borscht or chicken soup with pie for dessert was the dinner menu. Supper included cake

and red jello for dessert. Only important chores and milking were done on Sundays. We

often had visiting families for Sunday afternoon and they would stay for supper. Some

Sundays we went visiting neighboring farms.

The parishioners at Rosenthal and their peers in all churches in the area had

enormous faith in God. They believed in a just God, one who handed out punishment

as well as rewards, and they certainly strived for the latter. They professed utmost

respect for the church, the priests, nuns and all teachers. It was always like they knew

what was needed and worked to accomplish the task.

* * * * *

DAVID FERRIE

The Precious Blood Society priests whose Ohio high school seminary I attended

from 1941 - 1946, tended North Dakota parishes in Grassy Butte, Fayette, Killdeer,

Hazen, Dodge, Hebron, Hazelton, Linton, Rosenthal and Hague (the Creek) from 1921 -

1993. So when Shirley and I came to live in Dickinson in 1955 quite a few of these prairie pastors had been my schoolmates. They showed up frequently at our house and dental office as we renewed old school friendships. One day in November, 1963 one of them in great excitement scurried into the office holding a newspaper picture of a scar faced man flanked by police officers. "Do you recognize this guy?" he asked, bursting to tell me if I didn't. The name under the picture spelled David Ferrie, an airplane pilot arrested at a Dallas, Texas airport, and a former seminary schoolmate of ours. The newspaper went on to state that the scarred face had resulted from burns Ferrie had suffered in a plane crash while a World War II Air Force pilot. The priest and I remembered David Ferrie as a bright student with a big desire to be a priest but was expelled from the seminary.

On the day of his November 1963 arrest, Ferrie waited inside his parked plane, allegedly to fly Lee Harvey Oswald from Dallas after the assassination of President John F. Kennedy.

In the 1991 movie, "J.F.K.", depicting the assassination of President Kennedy, actor Joe Pesci played the character of David Ferrie. The screen play dramatized the self-admitted homosexual Ferrie as a looser and a disappointed ex-monk who was denied the opportunity to become a priest, having had to unwillingly leave the monastery.

* * * * *

A REPORTER'S LIFE

In a recent book, "A Reporter's Life", an autobiography by Walter Cronkite, people my age are given a review and clear story of the important historical events in their lifetime.

Cronkite began his journalism career writing for newspapers in the 1920's. With progression of radio he took to the air waves and climaxed his journey via television anchorman. His vivid word crafting tells of interviews with and stories of thirteen presidents from Coolidge to Clinton. He details battles in World War II, the Korean War, the Viet Nam War, Grenada, Panama and the Persian Gulf. He witnessed military invasions, lived in fox holes, flew on bombing missions, accompanied rescue ventures and visited prisoner of war camps. He spent time on ships where generals planned battle strategies. Cronkite tells of rifts between military and political leaders, of egotistical decisions, mistakes and friendly fire. He tells of blackouts, rations and victory gardens. He describes country leaders like Hitler, Stalin, Churchill, Saddam Hussein and more. He mentions fellow reporters Edward R. Murrow, Ernie Pyle, Lowell Thomas and more. Walter Cronkite was there and tells what he saw and what historians were to repeat.

On the home front Cronkite explains the crash of 1929, labor strikes, mafia groups, racial integration, Martin Lutheran King, the Kennedy assassination, presidential elections, the nuclear age, space age, DNA age, computer age, petrochemical age, Internet, poverty and more. He predicts an evolution, social, political and economic, with the explosiveness of a revolution and hopes to observe his forecasts "from a perch yet to be determined". People my age are fortunate to have had Walter Cronkite as a contemporary.

* * * * *

UNCLE FRANK JOSEPH HAGEL

I met an old friend, Tony Hagel, at the Dakota Pioneer Chapter of Germans from Russia meeting in Bismarck on March 25, 1997. The event was at the Burleigh County Senior Center where I read from *"My First World"* and several of my memory essays from the *Emmons County Record*. Tony is 17 years my senior, sharp as a tack and a walking history book of anyone and anything in "My First World." He recounts breaking me away from my pacifier when I was two years old. "That dirty thing, throw it away, you don't want to put that old thing into your mouth."

Tony brought memories of his dear father, lovingly known to me as Vetter Franz Sep (Uncle Franz Joseph). We had mutual affection. He was a warm, tender, portly man with a wide ready smile. Summers he never wore shoes, but to church, then tennis shoes. His callused feet withstood prairie barbs and thistles. He used sheep skin to quell the hot steel plate he stood on while driving the header during harvest. While fetching cattle on a windy day he dragged a long rope from his torso to help maintain balance. He frequently visited my house. "Don't you spank little Eddie," he counseled mother, as he came to my defense.

Vetter Franz Sep loved to play Whist. Spades were his favorite suit and the Ace of Spades his favorite card. I had a fond little nickname for him, "Shieba", (Spades). Once he was dealt his dream hand, a long Ace high run in Spades. As he laid each card he slammed it on the table and yelled, "Shieba". "Eddie, get me some cold water for my hand", as I hung on his chair.

One day in 1935 he died at age 55 of da bront (infection), they called it. There were many cars and horse teams at the wake and the house was crowded. I served Mass at the funeral. A Bosch they called "Yosel" brought the casket to the Rosenthal Church in his Model T truck. After Mass pallbearers Tony Bosch, Felix Stoppler, Paul Ibach, Pius Kelsch, Jack Schneider and a Bosch they called "Dox" carried the casket to the nearby cemetery. Father Henry Friedel, I, Joe Klein, Joe Vetter and the family followed close behind Vetter Franz Sep. The rest of the congregation followed. Tears fell into my mouth as we prayed for my friend, buddy and neighbor and as young men filled the grave with earth.

For months and years after Vetter Franz Sep's farm seemed only half there as I passed through it on my way to school.

* * * * *

SELLING MY DENTAL PRACTICE

Solo, 41 year dental practice, beautiful building designed as a dental building, three operatories, across from a large area hospital and medical clinics. University town, population 16,097, public and parochial grade and high schools, 50 miles drawing area, on I-94. Ranching, oil and manufacturing, good hunting and fishing, near Theodore Roosevelt National Park and Lake Sakakawea. Reasonable price and financing.

I sent this information along with color pictures of the building, waiting room and one operatory to all the dental schools in the United States. I also advertised this in the

National Dental Association Journal and in the Northwest Dentistry Journal for North Dakota and Minnesota. Dental practices are sold in three parts; the building, the practice and the equipment.

Most dentists retire at age 62. I have gone seven years beyond. I still love my work and am saddened to abandon those creative skills. But nature dictates different paths at different ages in our lives. I am looking forward to leisurely breakfasts as I now enjoy on weekends and more time to do as I please. That includes another creative urge I have, writing. Writing when you have the urge to write is more fun than writing when you can find time to write. There are quite a few things I feel the need of telling.

Maybe a young dentist from New York or California will take my place in Dickinson and our town will be better for it all. I have certainly enjoyed my 41 years as a dentist here.

Shirley is now 62 and has decreased the size of her work load in her home health nursing practice at St. Joseph's Hospital and Health Center. She enjoys flowers, her work with the Dickinson Forestry Committee and her P.E.O. Organization and, of course, her work.   * * * * *

BAKING COOKIES 1997

I baked cookies, my favorite kind, the quadruple major ingredient kind, chocolate chip, raisin, oatmeal and walnuts.

After blending margarine, brown sugar, white sugar, eggs, milk, vanilla, flour and baking soda into a velvety sleek mixture, I added the chocolate chips, raisins, oatmeal and walnuts. Twenty scoops of the batter on a tin in a 350° oven for ten minutes produced automatic results. I felt somewhat creative, even though I worked pretty hard, tripling the recipe.

Baking cookies gives me time to think of how my mother baked cookies in the 1930's at my farm home near Strasburg. For sure, she would never have indulged in four major ingredients in the same cookie batch---two at the very most. Without electricity the "blend" would have been hand powered and not so "velvety". With wood, chips and coal for fuel, the oven would not have been an even 350° and the ten minutes--- forget it. Constant observation was the rule. Yet the aroma from her cookie baking, my excitement of the occasion and the bountiful cookie display on the kitchen table afterward far exceeded the rapture I experienced from my indulging chocolate chip, raisin, oatmeal and walnut cookie baking yesterday.

The women in the 1930's were absolute baking phenoms with their wood, chip and coal fueled cook stoves.   * * * * *

STRASBURG'S BLUE ROOM

When the Chicago, Milwaukee and St. Paul Railroad erected a spur into Emmons County in 1902 businesses sprang up at the crossing and the town of Strasburg was born. Saints Peter and Paul Catholic Church at the community of Tiraspol by Carl Keller's farm moved into town. During the first six years something was missing in Strasburg. There was no Blue Room.

That changed in 1908 when Gregory Bichler built a bar and pool room, the forerunner of the ever popular Blue Room. For a time Bichler housed a liquor store there and also a bowling alley and later developed a dance floor. Public and wedding dances in the 1930's and early 1940's featured the great accordions of John Schwab, Mike Dosch, the Mastel Brothers, Tom Gutenburg, Charlie Richter and Sam and His City Fellers with their *Clarinet Polka* theme song. Anniversaries and other social gatherings happened there. Sometime later the facility became the Matt-Ray Lounge and Blue Room. After World War II, under the Mattern ownership, the Blue Room was increased in size for the dance floor and flourished as never before. Weddings abounded, twenty five in one thirty day stretch. Always adding to the popularity of the place were four other watering holes within a minutes walk to help service the large crowds.

Weddings were all day affairs. After the church ceremony a soup dinner at the Blue Room enhanced the celebrants and spirits flowed. Dancing erupted immediately after dinner till just before the opening of presents. Supper followed and then all cleared to the lounge for more refreshments before the wedding dance.

In 1949 the Matterns remodeled the Blue Room and added more feet of dance space. Indoor plumbing was added and no more kerosene stoves needed for cooking or water to be hauled in. Outdoor privies became obsolete and the Blue Room was state of the art. Much of North Dakota, Minnesota and South Dakota partook in festivities at the Blue Room. Local orchestras were complemented with the musical caliber of our-of-staters Whoopee John, the Six Fat Dutchmen and the Royal Kings. The local Bubbling Quintet began their sweet sounds. The Blue Room was in high gear. For 25 cents people enjoyed class entertainment. Basketball games, roller skating and movies satisfied the entertainment tastes of many in the Blue Room. Movies featured "Pal Night", two for the price of one. Murals of trees, lakes and rolling hills graced the walls as the woodwork on the bar and back bar rivaled the interior of the church in artistic splendor.

In 1970 the Horners purchased the Blue Room and Lounge and continued operations much the same. The dances never let up. Today the Carlsons operate the facility with little change in events and style but under a new name. They added rose paint and renamed the 88 year old entertainment palace The Rite Spot (as it has always been) and Rose Room.

The walls of the Rose Room contain many happy memories. A large percentage of married couples in Strasburg and for miles around courted and married there. With all the musical events held there Lawrence Welk's Champagne Music was never one of them---Welk's crowds always needed the high school gym.

* * * * *

AARP AND "*MODERN MATURITY*"

The American Association of Retired Persons, AARP, was founded in 1958 by Dr. Ethel Percy Andrus to better the lives of older Americans. Today 350,000 volunteers from 4,000 local chapters provide service, advocacy and education to promote health care and quality of life for older people. Volunteers explore workers' rights and retirement planning. Membership in AARP includes 32 million of the 68.2 million 50+ American adults. AARP tracks their changing behavioral patterns with up-to-date research.

Modern Maturity magazine is published by AARP every two months. It is circulated to the 32 million members as a benefit of the $8 annual membership fee. With its recent new design this reader friendly and entertaining publication continues to disseminate information for the nations largest organization of people 50 and over.

Americans today are living longer, retiring later, enjoying better health and leading more active lives than ever before. Only 10% of people over 65 have chronic health problems and less than 5% are in nursing homes. Mature Americans are no longer "settled" at 50 and retired at 65. Today the 50's decade is the most turbulent ten years in life. Psychologically 50's people feel 15 years younger and can expect to live another 29 years. Responsibility toward parents, grandchildren, and their own children returning home; divorce and remarriage and second families; mid-life crises; career changes and menopause all add to their life reassessments. The free birds, age 69, tend to be retired and freed from family obligations.

The following paragraphs contain facts obtained from "Re-defining Mature America," a new study prepared for AARP's *Modern Maturity* magazine by Roper Starch World-Wide Inc.

The average income of all 50+ Americans is $14,063. The majority of this money is from social security and pensions and most use credit cards and get their financial advice from bank officers.

Most mature Americans contribute to a church or synagogue and to community projects.

Reading and walking head the list of their hobbies.

Eating out and socializing with friends are by far the most popular entertainment activities.

What 50+ people want to know about most are new health care developments and current events.

Proper diet, exercise and recreation are very important, but these seniors have a difficult time resisting ice cream and as a group are the largest coffee drinkers in the United States.

Environmental concerns include the need for recycling paper and plastic products. They consider disposable diapers the top cause of solid waste problems.

Most seniors enjoy retirement years. Just 10% have jobs. Activities with grandchildren are a top priority. What they enjoy with them most is telephone conversations, meals and gift exchanging.

The most popular senior food is potatoes. Chicken/turkey and cereal are second and third. Coffee is the favorite drink.

To them cost of food is more important than nutritional content.

Seniors enjoy cotton to any other fiber for their apparel.

Eight out of ten older Americans are home owners.

They prefer to travel by car and airplane, stay in hotels and most often visit beaches, lakes and shores. They buy their cars with an eye toward safety and mileage.

Most have cable TV and VCR's, national news and game shows are their TV preferences.

Armed with research of this kind AARP educates and informs its messenger, *Modern Maturity*.

* * * * *

NATURAL CATASTROPHES

The two greatest natural catastrophes in the history of the middle west occurred on October 8th, 1871.

In densely forested northeastern Wisconsin near Preshtigo on the Green Bay, hunters, fisherman, Indians, lumberjacks, railworkers and farmers were building campfires, cutting lumber, fixing rails, clearing land and burning stumps. These activities were no different from the activities every fall in this region. Factories in Peshtigo and nearby Marinette were manufacturing anything from wooden boxes to wagon wheels to clothes pins. Boarding houses abounded with transient laborers to swell the population of Peshtigo to 1,700.

What was different about the fall of 1871 was its intense dryness. Other falls all had been wet. Already in September many small fires joining other small fires had to be extinguished with water wagons and pails. Some people became uneasy and dug extra wells by their homes. However the imminent danger was mostly ignored, people going about as usual. Fires became more numerous as the days went by. Smoke filled the skies and boats on Lake Michigan were forced to navigate with the use of compasses.

Early evening, October 8th, a west wind began churning the fires and the inferno was on. The winds became hurricanish and thunderous smoke balls bellowed from the crimson skies as the flames enveloped the trees and everything in their path. Houses exploded. The factories were on fire. Burning tree branches, dust, cinders, ashes, sparks, smoke, and hot air wouldn't let people open their eyes as they scampered and probed toward the Peshtigo River. Winds knocked people down to the ground and many were trampled. Horses, cows and dogs in total bewilderment were running about. The fortunate people who reached the river entered and submerged to their heads. They constantly splashed their heads to keep from burning. Trees and houses on both sides of the river were on fire forming a hellish dome over the water. The river saved the lives of the fortunate few who made it there. The water was full of burning logs, tree branches, horses, dogs and cows. People were seen hanging on to horns of the cows. People were in the river from 8 p.m. until 4 a.m. The fire ravaged 2,400 square miles from Peshtigo south to Green Bay (the city) and north to Escanaba, Michigan. One thousand people died, mostly all from Peshtigo where they were completely surrounded. Shirley's grandmother, Catherine Mcmillan Maloner, then age seven, was one of the people who survived in the river.

Governor Lucius Fairchild's office in Madison did not receive this horrible news until the morning of October 10th. All telegraph equipment had been ruined. On that day the governor was in Chicago helping out with the other middle west catastrophe. On the very same night of October 8th, a cow kicked a lantern in a Chicago barn and ignited a fire that destroyed the core of Chicago, three hundred lives and $200,000,000 of property. The same cyclonic winds prevailed in Chicago that night as had in Peshtigo, Wisconsin.

The Peshtigo fire never received the publicity that the Chicago fire did. In lives lost it was far greater. It was the worst forest fire in the history of the middle west. The Chicago fire was the most destructive in terms of city property and city lives lost.

* * * * *

SOUNDS OF THE EARLY PRAIRIES

Gullies and creeks gushed as April uncovered the fields and the hills of wintery white.   Squeaking gophers bade greetings as they crawled from hibernation. Meadowlarks sang from fence posts as farmers prepared seedbeds with horses hoofing through furrows of earth.   Over the hill the steady hammer of an engine told of a John Deere at work.

Baby calves and lambs cried, searching for their mothers. Mother hens clucked to protect their scampering young from a hovering hawk; little birds chirped in sharp maneuvers, taunting the hawk.

Lightning bolts and percussive thunder struck terror into children fetching cows for milking. Men working in the fields too feared the deadly strikes. Rain pattering on the roof of an attic bedroom was calming; smashing hail was hostile and howling winds threatened, shaking the house at night. Frogs gurgled "thanks yous" for the rain.

Miles away chug-chugging steam engines commanding a resounding whistle of the Soo Line, on time, carrying cream cans and orders for machinery parts, crawling to Ipswitch, South Dakota to meet the Milwaukee Road.

The clattering of wagon wheels or humming of Model T's hinted of guests before farm dogs confirmed their arrival. Blowing dust fell in banks after peppering the house. Fluttering hoppers with whirling wings moved in huge clouds and blotted out the sun as the dust had done, colliding against the barn. They fell in banks on the ground.

The shuttering windmill driving a squeaking waterpump begged the well not to go dry and sadden the awaiting stock tank. Shattering header blades fed a clattering canvas, conveying grain stocks to the header box. The deafening tractor's pulley powering a roaring threshing machine was background music to comaradering farmers. "Ho" and "Gitty-up" guided horses on grain wagons. Shrilling crickets filled the night.

Wild geese honked in perfect formations, (crows squawked in less perfect groups.) Shotguns and rifles pursuing pheasants and jacks palpitated the air.

High-pitched horse hooves sped over hardened snow keeping time to squeaking sleigh runners and rattling harnesses. Maytag engines banged to announce washday. Sunday church bells invited all to prayer, weekday bells told of someone called to his God. Far-a-way coyote howls seemed so near, intense rumbling in the sky revealed an airplane, an instant marvel.

And the sweetest sound of all, the dinner bell assembled all in cheerful union, thanking God for food and life.

This I remember; the nineteen-thirties; Emmons County; North Dakota; this was my home.   * * * * *

RETIREMENT PARTY

There was a retirement party at the Dickinson Elks Club, November 15, 1996, celebrating my 41 and a 1/2 years of dental practice.

When our children suggested a party my first reaction had been negative. I wanted no hoop-de-doo, and who would want to come to my party? But seven grown children in unison are convincing. They insisted and invoked terms like commitment and dedication, words invented long after we started a dental practice and a family. Shirley soon succumbed and I became jelly. Celebrants included our children, some spouses, one grandchild, dental colleagues, old college friends, long time Dickinson friends, relatives and Diana Hibl, a 25 year co-worker. We enjoyed a reception, refreshments and dinners of Chicken Cordon Bleu, Prime Rib and Walleye Pike, served for the eight tables in the elegant style of the Elks Club Rooms. Accolades seemingly routine at these events become highly charged when they are yours. Son, Tom left few doubts that our children learned many positives in the 41 and a 1/2 years. Life long friend Al Wolf talked about growing up together in "My First World" area. It brought me a tear when he spoke of the gracious hostess my mother was during church feast day celebrations . . . even mentioned his choice of apple or lemon meringue pie at our house. I never knew how good I made him feel being his friend over the years. St. Thomas College and long time friend Bill Foster, expounded on the persistence for progress Germans from Russia people posses.

Eleven-year-old grandson Weston concluded the celebration with more strokes for his grandma and grandpa, "In all the eleven years of my life grandma and grandpa have been very good to me."

As the evening concluded and I sat next to Shirley in my new blue suit, a life member American Dental Association pin on the lapel, my 1955 dental school graduation ring on my finger, in the midst of all my loved ones, I thought this celebration immensely appropriate. Events as these encourage young people and comfort mature people. Persistence, dedication and commitment are truly worthwhile terms. And I thank God I was there.

* * * * *

CATHOLIC NUNS IN NORTH DAKOTA

Catholic nuns played an impressive role in the development of North Dakota. The first Catholic nuns in North Dakota were in Pembina in 1853, 36 years before statehood. They were the Sisters of the Propagation of the Faith. The entire group was made up of Native American Indians and founded a school at St. Joseph's (now Walhalla) in 1854.

In the 1870's Benedictine Sisters from St. Joseph, Minnesota, founded St. Mary's School in Bismarck and later St. Alexius Hospital. These women today sponsor The University of Mary.

Presentation Sisters from Ireland opened St.Joseph's Academy in Fargo in 1882. This later became Sacred Heart Academy and today is Shanley High School. These sisters founded St.Orphanage in 1887 and provided health care in 1939.

Another American Indian sisterhood, The American Congregation, began at Elbowoods in 1891 and were known as the Red Sisters. They were headed by Sister Crowfeather, daughter of Chief Crowfeather, and founded a school and a hospital. Financial support was hard and some of them left the Order and the rest joined the American Army. Eventually they all returned to their families, got married and raised families.

A second group of Presentation Sisters arrived in Valley City in 1903 where they established schools and hospitals.

Also a second group of Benedictines came from Pennsylvania to Elbowoods in 1910 and took over the quarters left by the Native American nuns there. They established hospitals and schools in Garrison, Minot and finally Richardton.

Ursuline Sisters from Germany came to Strasburg in 1910 to establish a school there.

In 1912 Holy Cross Sisters from Germany established St. Joseph's Hospital in Dickinson and later a Practical School of Nursing there.

In 1928 Franciscan Sisters arrived at Hankinson. They opened a grade school in 1928 and a high school in 1930. They established a vestment factory, an elderly care facility in 1945 and a hospital in 1947.

Benedictine nuns from Indiana came to Belcourt in 1933 and established St. Ann's Mission School. In 1956 they established Queen of Peace Priory there.

School Sisters of Notre Dame came to New Hradec in 1917 and established a school. They are today still in New England and Dickinson.

In the 1940's Precious Blood Sisters from Ohio came to Linton and established a grade and high school.

Wahpeton was the site for an Order of Carmelite nuns in 1954. This was a cloistered contemplative Order devoted to prayer and meditation.

* * * * *

EARLY NORTH DAKOTA CATHOLIC SCHOOLS AND HOSPITALS

When the Lord enticed pioneer Sisters to early Dakota prairies, He played no favorites. They endured the same vast distances, sparse population, severe winters, dust storms, grasshoppers and economic depression as the settlers encountered. But the Sisters were keen in adapting to poverty and hardship to win the survival of their mission: education, health care and promoting the Catholic Faith. The great distance and often impassable roads required the schools to maintain boarding houses for children to stay overnight during the week. Not the elitist type boarding schools found in more affluent parts of the country for girls, these dormitories accommodated both boys and girls, rich and poor, where the Sisters conducted a family type atmosphere mixed with study, recreation, chores and prayer. Parents who could pay some money did so. The great majority of children took home lists of food on Fridays that they were to bring on Mondays. Milk, pork, flour, eggs, along with chickens, geese and ducks in gunny sacks, were regulars on the lists. Monday nights featured a butchering party starring the older children. The Sisters grew gardens and preserved for the winter. Children picked gardens after school.

Non-school farmers showed generosity to school menus. The parish church helped what it could with finances. Often the Sisters were paid nothing or $20/$30 per month for teaching. The Motherhouse depended on those dollars for existence. Musically talented Sisters gave lessons six day a week and directed adult choirs to complement income. Hospitals paid the Sisters more for their work. There they received the same salary as lay people. Hospitals enjoyed government grants and good private pay. The Sisters often used this health care money to supplement the schools. Fairs, bazaars, raffles and benefits of all kinds found their way to help schools. Public schools in some areas harvested the teaching talents of the Sisters. These areas were so predominately catholic that there were few students left to conduct a public school.

In the late 1950's North Dakota Sisterhoods provided for 31 high schools, 68 grade and junior high schools, 40 health care centers, eight nursing and retirement homes, three seminaries and colleges, two industrial schools and one orphanage. Plus they taught on weekends and in the summer children not in Catholic schools and children of migrant workers. The year 1965 saw 1,200 Sisters working in North Dakota.

The Sisters influenced North Dakota in education, health care, music, architecture (Marcel Breuer), foods (Johnnycake), folk art (church vestment making) and of course religion. History credits the church in general, or the Wherles and Shanleys and Martys for much of these accomplishments, but the trenches were filled with these "Queens of the Prairie". An even larger travesty reveals many of these now elderly women living in less than poverty in 1996.

* * * * *

SOME LESS KNOWN FACTS OF INTEREST

Cats have over one hundred vocal sounds, while dogs only about ten.

Our eyes are always the same size from birth, but our nose and ears never stop growing.

Montpelier, Vermont is the only U.S. state capital without a McDonalds.

The Pentagon in Arlington, Virginia has twice as many bathrooms as is necessary. When it was built in the 1940's the state of Virginia still had segregation requiring separate toilet facilities for blacks and whites.

There are two credit cards for every person in the United States.

In the last 4,000 years, no new animals have been domesticated.

Babies are born without knee caps. They don't appear until the child reaches two to six years of age.

49

Teeth are full size when they erupt.

The most common name in the world is Mohammed.

No NFL team which plays it's home games in a domed stadium has ever won a Superbowl.

The only two days of the year in which there are no professional sports games (MLB, NBA or NFL) are the day before and the day after the Major League All-Star Game.

Only one person in two million will live to be 116 or older.

* * * * *

MY ROCK PILE PLAYGROUND

When I was a little boy, during "My First World," a huge mound of rocks in a field just northeast of my house served as a dumping ground for farmyard and household castaways. Weasels and jackrabbits frolicked and nested there. Animal carcasses, long eaten clean by coyotes lay on those rocks. A chokecherry tree grew through its outer edge. Ancient glaciers left these rocks, ranging in size from softballs to boulders. To ready the land for plowing my father piled them up with horse teams and barges and wagons, as he toiled with worn gloves, aching arms and aching back.

Discarded buggy wheels and axles, worn horse collars, old harness pieces, baling wire (from bought hay), Model T steering wheels and rusted car bodies, old motors, tires and inner tubes, old lumber pieces, metal pipes, scrap iron, fruit and vegetable tins (some peas and beets still in tact), milk pails, syrup pails, wash tubs, pots and pans, knives,

50

forks and spoons, machinery parts, broken pitch forks, worn leather shoes, rusted stoves and broken wagon-trees all awaited my salvage skills.

From these treasures I made sleds wagons, skates and merry-go-rounds (putting a free-end axle into the ground like a fence post and riding the wheel on top). I made sling shots (the leather show tongue became the cradle for the projectiles, strips of inner tube rubber the slings, and little "Y" shaped branches from the chokecherry tree, the hand piece). The chokecherry tree provided a happy anticipation from spring green cherries to red cherries to black stained by juicy chokecherries.

Ashen white, sun cured animal skulls, some with horns and tooth filled jaw bones attached to spindly spine bones and leg bones with hooves, rested there. The ones with bits of fur I still recognized, like my horse friend, Tom, who couldn't digest the many thistles in '34 and the little Guernsey who couldn't calve in '35.

There was the day when my weasel traps tangled a skunk at the rock pile. I stayed a distance as my .22 ricocheted the rocks and brought down the malodorous cat. "Don't you ever come near this house," my mother shouted.

* * * * *

DENTAL INSURANCE

On an early 5 o'clock, frosty Saturday morning in January, I board a twin engine plane at the Dickinson Airport. Pilot Pat Giese heads for Bowman and we land. In the darkness a vague figure approaches and enters the plane, it's Dr. James Folske. Off we fly to the Hettinger Airport where we gather up banker Magnus Meyer and now we are heading for the Fargo Airport.

As we cross the Missouri River the sun begins to beam and soon sits whole on the far off snowy horizon, a magnificent orange ball of fire. I sat in the co-pilots chair. An instrument deploying a computer chip on the plane, one on a satellite and a third at the Fargo Airport tells us the exact distance to our destination. "This instrument was perfected in Desert Storm," the pilot informs me, "it applies a triangular theorem of mathematics." The pilot is friendly and makes conversation once we are in the air, but becomes strictly business for landing and take off. I like that.

Our flight is taking us to a 9 o'clock Dental Service Corporation board meeting at the Blue Cross Blue Shield building in Fargo. You see, in 1974 North Dakota dentists each volunteered $185 for a $25,000 pool to cover insurance claims of anticipated members. North Dakota Blue Cross Blue Shield administers this dental insurance plan with the able talents of Mr. Robert Carlson. The above mentioned pool is now $2,906,436 and the anticipated members number 165,654 North Dakotans.

The Dental Service Corporation board of directors is composed of dentists and lay people from across North Dakota. Board members from the western area use charter plane service to avoid car travel expenses and an overnight stay in Fargo.

After a 2-3 hour meeting and a toothsome lunch we wake our pilot at the Fargo Airport lounge. He swoops us over the Fargo flats and on over the lakes among the rolling plains and on to the buttes and pointed hills of Hettinger, Bowman and finally Dickinson.

The time is 3:30 p.m. and I'm home in my den enjoying a Saturday afternoon golf tournament on TV. * * * * *

CAPTAIN JAMES E. EMMONS

Emmons County was named after Captain James E. Emmons. Emmons was born in Virginia in 1843. He then moved to Nebraska. As a youngster he became a cabin boy on the Mississippi River and its tributaries. In 1865, during the Civil War, he engaged in federal river transportation work and this led him to the Dakotas.

Captain Emmons fought Indians at the mouth of Dry Forks of the Little Missouri River. There he lost four men on the boat "Effie Deans."

Emmons established the first ferry between Bismarck and Fort Lincoln but had to sell out after one season in 1877. In the 1870's he operated various businesses in Bismarck. At one time he was poet trader at Camp Hancock. There he was in charge of a stock goods owned by Hohn J. Charles of Sioux City.

A true pioneer, Captain Emmons was the first settler of Edwinton (later Bismarck). He had one of the first businesses there and built one of the first brick blocks in Bismarck. He also brought the first bride to Bismarck. Her name was Nina B. Burnham of Yankton, South Dakota. Nina came on the first steamboat to reach Bismarck after the Northern Pacific built the crossing of the Missouri River. Mrs. Emmons was one of the founders of the North Dakota Historical Society.

To continue Captain Emmons' string of firsts, he became the father of the first born child in Bismarck. The first *Bismarck Tribune* ever printed was bought by Emmons. His steamboating to Dakota on the Missouri was a constant source for supplies to Indian trading posts and mines. Emmons County was named after a river rat and settled by land rovers.   * * * * *

53

THE GI BILL

How did your Strasburg farmer father ever get the money to pay for your eight years of college in the late 1940's and early 1950's. I faced this frequent inquiry over the years. The answer is, the GI Bill of Rights. After World War II between 1946 and 1956 the U.S. Government invoked a Bill, sending two million veterans to college which caused an astounding revolution in American education, colleges filled over the brim with the best students this country had ever seen.

The GI Bill also trained 3.5 million veterans in other schools, 1.4 million in on-the-job training and 690,000 in farm training. And it paid off handsomely. Economists calculate that during the lifetime of the average veteran, the U.S. Treasury received two to eight times as much in income taxes as it paid out in education benefits.

GI Bill recipients received $65 a month (married $90 and disabled more) plus all tuition, books and fees. Nearly half of all college students were veterans. Young non-vet freshman found themselves seated next to battle toughened men who had defeated Hitler and Tojo. Classroom competition was fierce.

In late 1945 I was 18 years old and draft eligible when a recruiter offered the Dwight D. Eisenhower plan---thirty-six months of service yielded thirty six months of college plus twelve months bonus---forty-eight months of college for three years of service---most fair. In 1948 I was at St. Thomas College in St. Paul, Minnesota. Veterans were exempt from freshman initiation. Seventeen year old freshmen Strasburgers Al Wolf, Jimmy Wickenheiser and Syl Schumacher looked silly in their freshmen beanies. I enjoyed playing on the Nodak intramural basketball team with them, especially during the rare times when Wolf relinquished the ball. The veteran classmates were simply impressive. My ex-Marine physics teacher, James Dolan, working on his Ph.D at the University of Minnesota, knelt on the floor during our opening class prayers. Later at Marquette University Dental School classmate 37 year-old Thomas Griffey had commanded a war ship in the South Pacific. Another dentistry schoolmate, Moris Bonnemeyer a long time dentist in Fargo, was plagued with shell shock attacks. These men were mature beyond their years, absolutely thankful to be alive and happy to be in school.

To supplement my GI Bill income I spent the six weeks between summer school and September pitching header boxes on brother Debert's farm at Strasburg, and wheat stacks with Bauman's threshing crew. I ate five great meals a day, slept on clean beds with a roomful of dirty guys. During the school year I sold shoes on weekends and took the night shift sometimes in the breweries ($2.50 an hour). I also found time to court an Irish Catholic nursing student, Shirley Maloney, heeding my mother's advice to come home married and not to dance with Lutherans. Now I am rambling into material here that will encompass "*My Second World*" down the road. But I will ever be grateful for the GI Bill of Rights and for the brave men who fought and died (men like Tony Bauman and Matt Schwab from "My First World" area) so the rest of us could have the GI Bill of Rights.   * * * * *

CHICKEN

Chicken today is the cheapest form of quality animal protein on the market. It wasn't always that way, however. In 1914 restaurant menus featured chicken somewhere between porterhouse and caviar. A candy bar advertised itself "Chicken Dinner." Politicians harvested the connotation by promising a chicken in every pot.

Chickens came from eastern Asia and Africa. Roosters were the symbols of dawn and aggressive behavior (cock fights). Hens symbolized much that is maternal and feminine or tender.

In ancient history war vessels harbored chickens for their supposedly inherent qualities to foretell sailors when to attack. If they ate well it was a sign to do battle. But the sailors soon became aware of the little space the birds required and how good their meat and eggs tasted.

Chickens arrived in America about 1600 and were admired for their self sufficiency. They fed on spilled grain, bugs, worms and table scraps and roosted in trees. White birds were unpopular because of being easily spotted by predators. Chickens laid about 30 eggs, mostly in the spring, which were hunted by wives for "egg money." Production was a farm amateur affair till 1877 when Jacobs Graves patented an incubator and offered two to four week old chicks for sale. A Mrs. Wilmer Steele from Delmarva Peninsula near Chesapeake Bay ordered 500 chicks and sold the surviving 387 for a whopping 62¢ a pound ($10 per pound in 1994 money).

In 1891 Cornell University became the first agricultural college to offer poultry husbandry and chicken production became commercial. Hatcheries grew from 250 in 1918 to 10,000 in 1927 and chicken went from a luxury to a daily food. Along with genetic engineering and bigger and better birds came more aggressive behavior. Upper bills were partially removed to avoid deadly pecking.

Technology, genetics and decreases in the use of manpower made profits possible. A state of the art hen house today is 100,000 birds, the length of two football fields with eggs rolling down onto conveyer belts and whisked away for cleaning, grading and packing. The only thing not automated is the removal of the 3 in 10,000 daily deaths.

Today we consume in the United States more chicken than beef. The Delmarva Peninsula and Arkansas are the two biggest area producers. Chicken costs a fraction of the price Mrs. Wilmer Steele received 200 years ago thanks to farmers, feed-mill owners, breeders, transporters, scientists, bankers and wholesalers.

* * * * *

UPDATE ON "*MY FIRST WORLD*"

Since Allan Burke, your editor, first reviewed "*My First World*" in the *Emmons County Record* about a year ago, many positives have happened to the book. There are presently 1,200 copies in print, 800 sold, 200 given away to newspapers and other publications and 200 in inventory.

"*My First World*" is enjoyed in almost every state in the U.S. plus Canada (and Egypt). North Dakotans, ex-Dakotans, Welk fans, pioneers and ethnic groups all identify with the many characters in the book. Newspapers in North Dakota, South Dakota, Minnesota, Montana, Iowa, Wisconsin, Kansas, Nebraska, Arizona, Washington, Oregon, California and Colorado have written reviews or stories about "*My First World.*" the *North Dakota Horizons* magazine, the *North Dakota Rural Electric Cooperative* magazine, *Senior Lifestyles of Bismarck*, and the *South Dakota* magazine are some other publications where "*My First World*" has found reviews. Historical Societies in North

Dakota and Minnesota and libraries in North Dakota, South Dakota, Minnesota and California have obtained the book. The North Dakota State Public Library had obtained permission to put the contents of the book on tape for people with impaired vision.

I have read and signed "*My First World*" copies for people in Dickinson, Williston, Bismarck, Grand Forks, Linton, Strasburg, Sioux Falls, South Dakota, the North Dakota State Library Convention in Bismarck and the International Reading Association Conference in Bismarck. I have read the book to teachers taking college courses and they are interested in reading or having me read the book to 4th and 8th grade North Dakota History classes.

I am giving reading presentations at 55+ meetings around the state, have shown "*My First World*" at art shows and sold it at ethnic celebrations around the state. In my collection are 400 letters, cards, and phone calls of "thank yous" for writing this book. People like to be given back a little piece of their childhood for a while. We all have a "first world". Memories are like flower petals. They preserve when pressed on paper. People come and go. The land remains. Each adds and takes from it---as the sun forever returns.

I am thrilled at the acceptance and the appreciation, and am so encouraged and happy to write more.

"*My First World*" with a map of all the farms, Linton and Strasburg can be reviewed on the Internet at http:/www.uccc.com/first world, a Father's Day gift to me.

* * * * *

THE WORLD OCEAN

The ocean is much larger than most people think. In fact the ocean makes up more than two-thirds of the earth . . . the rest is land. The world ocean is a confluence of the Pacific, Atlantic, Indian and Arctic Oceans. Of these four the Pacific Ocean is larger than the other three combined and much deeper. It extends half way around the world.

We hear the term "sea." A sea is the part of the ocean surrounded by land, like the Black Sea, where the people in "*My First World*" came from.

The Mediterranean Sea is between Africa and Europe, for example.

Ocean water is salty. The salt comes from rocks on the land, washed by rain into rivers flowing into the sea and ocean. The Red Sea is not really red. It only appears so because of the millions of tiny red algae plants that grow in the water.

The ocean has been a roadway for travel from country to country for thousands of years. Ferdinand Magellan set off from Spain 477 years ago with a fleet of five ships to sail around the world. Although he was killed on the way, one ship and 18 men completed the trip. They were on the ocean for three years.

* * * * *

CHRISTMAS IN THE 1930'S IN EMMONS COUNTY

In the 1930's we Germans from Russia at Rosenthal Sacred Heart Church community celebrated Christmas in a tradition that originated in Germany and survived through Russia.

On Christmas Eve Belza Nichol and Christkind visited our farms. Belza Nichol appeared as a rugged looking gentleman in a big inside out fur coat with a black belt, a mask on his face, black boots and a chain in his heavily gloved hands. He carefully observed our children's behavior, consulted with our parents, gave treats to those who had behaved and threatened to carry away in chains the ones who had not behaved.

Christkind, in white robes with a golden crown and golden wings, sat on a makeshift donkey. We children were asked to approach Christkind. Christkind offered us treats with one hand while threatening to hit us with a twig from the other hand. Most of us children ended up crying during the visit by these two characters who always came together. Everybody ended up receiving treats, however I could never figure the psychology here, but it did stress good behavior.

The second part of Christmas Eve proved much more delightful. Sacred Heart Church was illuminated with gas mantle lamps and tiny Christmas tree candles for midnight Mass. The splendor of the high altar, side altars, statues and pictures showed brilliantly among the mantle lamps. The Christmas tree, adorned with colorful glass hangings and candles, was simply awesome to me. The choir and pump organ enchanting "*Silent Night*" in German left little to my imagination. In my child's eyes I could almost see heaven. After Mass the priest had treats for us Mass server boys.

At home after church we had a special lunch that featured a traditional delicacy of pickled pigs feet and finally to bed.

My grandmother, Mrs. Wendelin Klein, always treated me at Christmas time with a sack of candy and nuts and a quarter wrapped in tinfoil among them. The most memorable Christmas gift I ever received as a child from my parents was a set of rubber stamps of the alphabet with an ink pad to print words.

* * * * *

RABBIT HUNT

As a freshman high school student at my seminary high school in Canton, Ohio in 1941, many school activities were totally unfamiliar. Free days were always announced the morning of and sometimes coincided with farm work, like potato picking time.

One hundred boys swarmed onto a 30 acre field to gather potatoes behind a digger and load them onto a wagon, to be hauled and unloaded into the sub-basement along side the apples, pears, carrots, egg plant, kohlrabi, beets, onions, pumpkins and squash.

But on this November free day the rector called for a rabbit hunt. I thought my gosh, a rabbit hunt? In Emmons County, North Dakota my father allowed me a .22 rifle to hunt jackrabbits, but any kind of fire power in the hands of my friends from New York, New Jersey and Illinois could prove more dangerous to hunters than to the hunted. Plus these Ohio hares were bunny rabbits, much smaller targets than North Dakota jacks. What kind of a rabbit hunt was going to happen here I thought?

My gun fire fears were alleviated when all 100 of us armed ourselves with sticks the size of baseball bats.

Our 400 acre seminary farm covered rolling hills and dales, generously sprinkled with five to six acre tree clusters. One hundred stickarmed, anxious combatants encircled a cluster and slowly converged toward the center. We clubbed our prey and they became more and more alarmed, darting in all directions as the arena became extinct.

However, not all the bunnies fell victim. Some of the speedy little critters, changing directions at the blink of an eye, embarrassed us hunters as they scampered to freedom through our forked-out legs.

A good day's hunt netted 100 rabbits. The nuns were most happy to reward our efforts in the refectory supper the next evening.

With readers who may think this 1941 sport to be inhumane to animals, I may agree. However, these little bunnies may not yet be out of the woods. Today the once hallowed 400 acres of seminary farm land and bunny habitat are an 18 hole Jack Nicholas designed golf course, the Glenmoor Country Club.

* * * * *

DENTAL HYGIENE

I teach dental hygiene to everyone in my practice. The condition of teeth and gums play a major roll in the overall health of the body.

Bacterial infection causes tooth decay and gum disease. The purpose of dental hygiene is to maintain a bacterial infection-free mouth.

The mouth, especially during sleeping, is an ideal place for bacteria to grow. In order for bacteria to grow in a medium there must be five conditions present. There must be moisture, warmth, darkness, food and no air. All of these are present in a closed mouth. If any one of these conditions is removed bacteria will not grow. Yep, you guessed it, we can take the food away.

The bacterial food is removed by brushing and flossing teeth and gums before bedtime. Also, during the night, a sticky substance forms on the teeth which can be removed before breakfast and spare the teeth from food sticking to them.

A good brushing technique is as follows: Place the brush as far back as possible on the cheek side of the lower left teeth. With the brush going in a circular motion move slowly forward on the line between the teeth and the gums. When the right side is reached flip the brush over to the tongue side of the teeth and work back to the left side. Now brush the top of the tongue and proceed the same way on the upper teeth . Brush the roof of the mouth and the job is done.

Flossing should be called wiping, because that is what is being done. Wipe the in-between sides of the teeth with floss; pushing down all the way to the gums on one tooth and up on the other.

So briefly, brush before breakfast and wipe with floss before bedtime . . . and then let's see what the bacteria will have for lunch.

* * * * *

MY FARM HOUSE

Before 1935 "My First World" house was a rectangular, flat roofed, one story frame structure with a lean to the same size. There was a "foreheisel" built on the entry of the latter for coats, boots, caps, kerosene stove, Maytag washer, cream separator and milk pails. The rest of the lean-to was the cooking, eating and sitting area plus the pantry with a hanging drape door. The pantry doubled, with a roll-away, as a bedroom for my two older brothers. A portion of its floor was the entry to the cellar. My fear always was the lid breaking or becoming undone and spilling people down the opening. "I'm going down the cellar, don't anyone come into the pantry," was often a warning cry. The steps were boards fitted onto, down and over notches sawed into two planks. The dungeon-like room below had an earthen floor and walls and a danky, musty smell. Potatoes, often sprouting toward spring, lay in one corner. Jars of pickles, beets, carrots, chokecherry jam and meat rested on apple crate shelves against the walls. There was a wooden crock of brewed raisin wine. Brewed malt beer and root beer were under the steps. A farmer match provided light for short visits and a kerosene lantern for the longer ones. The rectangular flat roofed portion housed the "shtoop," a slick-waxed linoleumed room with nicely papered walls and white crocheted-like curtains for the windows. It had a heating stove and a varnished wooden "shonk" bed, which was a tall dresser with a pull-down bed for my sisters. There was an oval built-in mirror at the top with bowls of wax fruit and family pictures resting on dollies on the dresser. Large oval framed pictures of the Sacred Heart of Jesus, grandparents and of my father during World War I graced the walls of the "shtoop," a room reserved for company. Off this room was a curtain-doored bedroom for my mother and father shared by my little brother and me, where in my "pretend sleep" I learned interesting sides of relatives and neighbors.

In 1935 my father, with the help of neighbors and carpenter Peter Moser from Strasburg built an upstairs to the rectangular flat roofed portion and all six children had a bedroom. My mother bought beds at an auction, deliced them with kerosene and filled three large canvas-type sacks with corn husks for mattresses. The sole heat source to the new bedroom was the open door below, but I supplemented by wearing a sheepskin coat, cap and stockings to bed in the 40 below weather. "Are you warm up there?" came the nightly call from my father as he re-entered the house with his lantern after the final feeding of the horses and cattle in the barn. The shingle nails peeking through the unfinished roof formed snowy frost balls from my breath.

Every fall my father winterized the house by piling earth knee high all around the foundation and stuffing rags into every crack possible around the window frames and door. During the thunder and rain storms not all the water inside the house was my mother's Holy Water---there were a few leaks in the roof now and then.

* * * * *

SKATING PARTY

Dressed in snowsuits and clutching ice skates ten 5-11 year olds piled into the 1967 yellow Dodge station wagon. Only the front seat was up giving the real wagon effect. Five year old Joey Keller didn't have skates but he had his little sled and was going to be pulled on the ice all the way to the other side. There was Denny and Dougie Braun, Allen and Mike Lynch, Ed, Ann, John, Mary and Tommy Keller. Their faces were full of cheer and they were putting on their skates as we headed to the Dickinson Golf Course with its snaking Heart River.

This sunny, windless December 12th, 1969 Saturday afternoon had been preceded by snowless, cold and calm days. The ice on the Heart River sported a glassy four inch thick gliding surface. Excitement was sky level as the throng piled onto the inviting river. I led the surge and as I continued around the first bend I heard Eleanor Sax, who lived near the river, "You have your hands full today, don't you?" It wasn't clear to me what she meant. I was so enjoying the kids having fun.

Suddenly, as if Eleanor's remarks had been a forewarning, John and Tommy came racing around the bend, screaming, "Ann is in the water and holding Joey." My mind shifted into a gear I had never ever experienced. I more than raced back to find Ann treading water in an open three foot wide air hole. She was pressing Joey to her body with one arm while trying to keep afloat with the other arm. She had been pulling Joey on his sled and he fell in after her. I saw the snowsuits taking on water and Ann's skates bearing weight. Both of their faces were full of fright with jarred open eyes. "Get us out," she yelled. I laid myself flat on the ice, inched to the hole, extended my right arm and snatched Joey into the air over my head. Then it was Ann's turn and with the same result, never realizing a strain or any weight on my arm; just slick movements and no doubts as to the outcome. Thank you adrenaline!

With glaring eyes and pale faces all the children gathered into the station wagon--- minus one sled. It wasn't until Joey and Ann were in a warm bathtub that tears flowed and flowed. "What were you thinking in the water Joey?" I asked. "I thought no Christmas presents," came the tearfilled voice. I have never forgotten what a heroine Ann Keller was that afternoon.   * * * * *

A VISIT TO "MY FIRST WORLD" COUNTRY

This past June 29th and 30th Shirley and I revisited "My First World" country in Strasburg. On this weekend the descendants of Ludwig and Christina Welk's children,

John, Barbara, Anna Mary, Louie, Agatha, Lawrence, Michael and Eva (the only living child) celebrated their once in every four year reunion. Present were 400 celebrants from 20 different states. Various colors representing each of the eight family tree branches brightened up the decor in the Blue Room as we mingled during supper and dance.

Strasburg was alive this Saturday night. In addition to the Welk group a wedding dance rang out from the KC Hall. A third dance in the street capped off the rodeo that day. Two high school class reunions complemented all three dances. An estimated crowd of 1,200 engulfed a three block area of downtown, consuming hundreds of brats and burgers served by the Pin Palace, washing them down with cases of milk, grape juice and pop.

All area motel rooms were filled for the night. Shirley and I were fortunate to secure a room at the Magnus Heidrich home which lived up to its name (Magnus is Latin for great).

Sunday morning breakfast at the Pin Palace presented the two largest hot cakes we ever saw. They were twelve inches in diameter and an inch thick. That along with a caramel roll, two eggs, two juices and two coffees for $5.70 had to be the bargain of the year. The Pin Palace man had worked 19 hours straight and the street fronting his business was void of any sign of party the night before.

Mass at Saints Peter & Paul Catholic Church with Sister Rose and Father Eckroth was packed. As usual the beauty and splendor of the church was breath taking and was complemented by two angelic little girls singing and playing guitars.

We spent the afternoon at the Lawrence Welk Homestead Museum picnicking with the reunionists, visiting with the frequent daily tourists from many states and signing "*My First World*" books.

In communicating with newspaper people around the United States while marketing "*My First World*" the name Strasburg lights up writers and turns them into next door neighbors. Strasburg is indeed the most well known small town in the United States.

Strasburg has never looked better. We congratulate its citizens for the tidy, painted houses and store fronts and the trimmed lawns and flowers. We congratulate Cindy Schatz for the great job she did in organizing the Welk reunion. Strasburg is a treat for visitors.   * * * * *

WATER WELLS

Many times water was hard to find on "My First World" farms. And often there was no money to hire a well driller. So people just dug the wells.

On a horseback ride to school on a September morning in 1937, approaching Wendelin Klein's farm near school I noticed Wendelin, his wife, Bridget, and neighbors Tony and John Hagel huddled with shovels in hand preparing to dig the ground. As I reined Bessy from her path and into a trot to check what they were up to, the 17 year old pony stumbled onto her front knees. I, along with the syrup lunch pail and school bag, tumbled to the ground. The Kleins and their neighbors dropped their shovels and came to the rescue, prodded Bessy to her feet and inspected her damage. The pail cover had come off but the syrup sandwich was holding and the two hard boiled eggs uncracked. They gathered up the books and helped me onto the pony. They told me of their plans to dig a well. I saw the prepared scaffolding with pulley, rope and sharp rimmed bucket to retrieve the dirt from the hole. Wells were sometimes 20-30 feet deep. How I wished I could have spent the day with them. That night as I hurried near the sight and saw the huge pile of dirt I knew they were close to finishing. They had gone 22 feet and were just bringing up Bridget with the pulley. She had a bandage around her head and a few droplets of dried blood on her face. "What happened to gettle? (Bridget was my godmother)" I asked. "Da batschich ox doha," she said, pointing to her husband, calling him a clumsy ox. Wendelin had accidently dropped the empty bucket into the hole. They had brought her to the surface before to bandage her wound.

You see, as the 5 foot by 5 foot square digging began all four diggers had room to work. As they penetrated the earth the future well narrowed to three, then to two and finally there was room for only the littlest digger, godmother. The bucket was filled below and pulled to the surface. As Bridget filled her last bucket of dirt, water from the underground springs spilled into the hole. Now it was her turn to exit the well. She climbed onto the bucket, one hand clinging on to her shovel, the other hand clutching a candle. (At certain depths a candle needed to burn off gases). The happy crew had found water and were preparing to build a square wooden well casing. But the next morning, passing through the Klein farm, I saw Wendelin witching for water from another area. The springs in the well the day before were poor and yielded only 1 1/2 feet of water.

* * * * *

THE CHICAGO BEARS

While viewing a National Football League game on television I thought back to my experience with the 1945 Chicago Bears training camp at St. Joseph's College in Rensselaer, Indiana. I had just graduated from high school and was attending summer session there when a classmate Tony Spitzig and I were asked to be food servers for the Bears training table. It was a welcome opportunity to see and meet the football players. They sometimes appeared beaten up. With no face masks and small tight-fitting thin leather helmets their faces often showed bruises and plenty of missing teeth. They were polite and kind to us servers. We had what they wanted---food.

The 1945 Bears roster contained 33 players, two co-coaches, one assistant coach and one trainer. George Halas, the president, owner and head coach was still in the United States Navy for World War II and was seldom at camp. There were five playing positions on the team; guard, tackle, end, center and back. People played both offense and defense. The heaviest player on the team was 6' 3" 246 pound center, Forest Masterson. The lightest player was also center, 6' 3" 165 pound, Joe Scheichl. Only 15 players weighed more than 200 pounds. Sid Luckman was the quarterback. Ed Sprinkle was a 6' 1" 190 pound tackle. Incidentally, Sprinkle plays in the Roger Maris Annual Charity Golf Tournament in Fargo every year. A couple years ago I had the pleasure to reminisce the 1945 Chicago Bears football team with Ed.

The NFL commissioner in 1945 was a former member of Notre Dame's famous Four Horsemen, Elmer Laden.

The ten game Chicago Bears playing schedule in 1945 started September 30th and ended December 2nd. It included home and away games with the Green Bay Packers, the Cleveland Rams, the Detroit Lions and the Chicago Cardinals. They played an away game with the Washington Redskins and a home game with the Pittsburgh Steelers.

These teams have been in existence long before 1945. The Cardinals won the NFL Championship in 1925, the Packers in 1929, the Bears in 1932 and the Lions in 1935. The Steelers never won a championship until 1974. From 1920-1932 the NFL championship was determined by a win-loss percentage. The first championship play-off game happened in 1933 and was won by the Bears.

During the final meal of the training camp the coaches made it known that the table servers deserved a tip for their fine work. This resulted in $68. But since community spirit prevailed in the seminary, our prefect intercepted the cash for a student body picnic. The Chicago Bears enjoyed a number of training camps at St. Joseph's College. This is evidenced by George Halas Hall on the campus.

* * * * *

SIMILARITIES OF TWO PAST EMMONS COUNTY STALWARTS

The similarities of two Emmons County pioneers who left impressive legacies in North Dakota history are significant. One of them, Lawrence Welk, needs little explanation. The other is my uncle, Louis Schneider, the last iron cross maker. The book *Iron Spirits*, by North Dakota Council On Arts, features Uncle Louis on page 57.

Louis Schneider 1901-1987 and Lawrence Welk 1903-1992 were contemporaries.

They were both born in Emmons County. They both married girls from St. Anthony, Rose Thomas Schneider and Fern Renner Welk. Both of their early ancestors were born in Winzenbach, Alsace, Germany. They migrated to Strasborg, Russia, and then to the Hague and Strasburg area in Emmoms County. Their fathers, Tibertious Schneider and Ludwig Welk were both blacksmiths. Ludwig often visited in the Schneider home. They were both talented as youngsters although neither had a formal education past the 4th or 5th grade. Louis learned blacksmithing in his father's shop and by the age of 16 was forging wrought iron crosses for cemetery grave markers in Hague, Strasburg, Linton, Mandan or wherever there were Germans from Russia. Lawrence became an accomplished musician at a very early age and played his accordion for many local dances and parties.

Both men left Emmons County in the 1920's. Lawrence went to South Dakota to pursue his music and Louis crossed the river to Fort Yates in Sioux County where he operated a blacksmith shop on the Standing Rock Indian Reservation. Huge portions of reservation acreage had been opened by the government to white buyers. Land-hungry Germans from Russia moved to Sioux County. Uncle Louis fixed wagons and sharpened plowshares for Indians and whites alike. The first iron cross he made on the reservation was for the grave of an Indian. It took five to seven days to make a cross and he charged $20. Louis endeared himself to the Indians, made many friends and became fluent in their Lakota language. The "Long Hairs" lined the walls of his shop and watched him perform his art. At times he lit their long stemmed pipes with a red-hot poker. They called him Mazakaga, which means cross maker, and shared many humorous and pre-reservation stories. They enjoyed seeing his large frame, massive hands and long powerful arms swing ten pound hammers, sometimes so hard that anvils broke. Whenever the Indians saw Louis make a cross they immediately inquired, "Who died?" or "Who is dying?" Eventually he tried to make crosses out of their sight since they superstitiously thought that this precipitated death. Uncle Louis respected everyone's feelings. As Lawrence was extremely popular and had many fans. Louis pleased whites and Indians alike and was elected Sheriff of Sioux County for 25 years. Uncle Louis spoke three languages, English, German and Lakota. He was a peacemaker between whites and whites, Indians and Indians and whites and Indians. His motto was, "Let's talk about this." Physical force was his very last resort.

Louis personally knew William P. Zahn (a former Army scout of George A. Custer), pioneer missionary Father Bernard Straussmaier, frontier photographer, Frank Fiske, and horse wrangler, Moustache Maude (Clara Bell Rose-Black).

I was acquainted with both men, Lawrence Welk and Louis Schneider. Both men possessed large friendly smiles, honest forthright demeanors, earn-it-yourself work ethic, unprejudiced innocence and loads of charisma. As a little boy on Sundays about once a year, I crossed the river in a rickety steam ferryboat with my parents to visit Uncle Louis. He was a kind, mellow man and made me feel special. To my childhood mind he seemed so out of place in a white Sunday shirt. It seemed he should be dressed like a blacksmith. As the similarities between the two men continue, in the 1940s Lawrence's niece, Alice Welk, married Louis' nephew, Debert Keller. And again Lawrence's nephew, Al Mattern, married Louis' niece, Mary Keller.

Louis Schneider's humility, respect for life, love of nature and the Plains Indians and all his friends and neighbors were evident at his funeral at St. Peter's Church in Fort Yates. The casket bore bright flowers and a Sioux Indian headdress. The choir intoned Sioux Indian hymns including Uncle Louis's favorite song, "*Yutipi Wakan Icupi Ichan*" (*Oh Lord I Am Not Worthy*).   * * * * *

HARRIET'S STORY

The following was written by Harriet Olson, a retired school teacher who lives in Dickinson. Harriet was in high school when this happened in Dickinson in 1935.

The July day was white hot and still - no wind - no noise at all. "Hurry and shut the windows," my mother called as she ran upstairs to do just that.

Suddenly, looking out to the east the sun was blotted out by a hugh cloud of black, buzzing, hissing "things". They completely obliterated the sun and covered everything I could see. The windows and screens were covered and the buzzing was deafening. Hundreds of the creatures bumped the house and fell to the sidewalk, which was littered with black, crunchy bodies. The cloud continued flying west - the numbers lying about did not seem to diminish the onslaught of that hissing, buzzing cloud. The flight was swift to the west, thousands dropping onto anything edible - the hemp clothesline disappeared and the green plants in the yard vanished. The hord continued moving west again.

When mom and dad opened the back door and we went outside it was horrid - we walked on and crushed bodies of grasshoppers two or more inches deep. Late movers flew swiftly to catch the main cloud, but there was nothing left for them to eat - the land was devastated and empty - the streets and yards were inches deep in dead grasshoppers.

All the neighbors emerged and swept or shoveled the refuse into cans, wheelbarrows or wagons. The city sent out road grades to clear streets!

Yes, in twenty minutes our lives were profoundly changed - not a living green thing remained, trees were denuded, lawns either consumed or black with bodies.

That year the crops in a wide swath disappeared as if by magic. The Biblical story of Egypt's locust infestation became very understandable. I had seen it happen in North Dakota.

* * * * *

THE WATKINS MAN

In "My First World" time I loved to hear the sudden dog barks, indicating a stranger approaching my farm. All visitors excited me, whether a neighbor borrowing sugar or coffee, someone on a pony searching for strayed horses or a wandering bull, or an "agent" peddling insurance (sometimes leaving gates open). Maybe a neighbor boy selling garden seeds, or some kid wanting to skate or swim at my dam, or just a neighboring couple for company. All these were welcome interruptions to my daily living. I loved lingering tobacco smoke after some left. The smell reminded me of company.

But the very favorite visitor was the Watkins man, a nice man named John Nicolai. When his blue 1929 four door Chevy with a rear custom trunk appeared over my east hill pasture trail, chills trickled down my back and excitement overtook me. He drove slowly to the front of my house, not to run over any chickens or children.

75

"Hello, children, here is a stick of Black Jack gum." "Is your mother home?"
"Tell him to come in," she yelled from inside the house. From his black suitcase satchel
he displayed bottles of liniment, camphor salve, carbolic salve, nectar extracts of orange,
lime, cherry and raspberry, Ludens cough drops, baking soda, vanilla, ginger, cinnamon,
pepper, bay leaves, fly spray, potato plant bug spray and powder and cow medicine. The
aroma was like a drug store.

If mother was short of cash the Watkins man accepted live chickens. I helped put
them into a gunny sack, which he furnished and they joined the cackling gang already
inside the trunk of his car.

On the days of the Watkins man, my father would arrive home from working in
the field and seeing my Black Jack gum, his thrifty side came alive, "Was he here
again?" "What did she buy this time?"

* * * * *

MEMORY OF AN EARLY TRAGEDY

I was away from home in 1946 when my sister announced her upcoming wedding.
I asked my mother to tell me about the prospective in-law. "He's a Mattern boy from
Strasburg she met two years ago at the Blue Room while he was home from the war,"
she said, "and he is a nice boy. He has such a nice smile and looks like his uncle
Lawrence Welk. He has a 1941 Buick with a 400 horse motor that can plunge through
every snow bank in our yard and plans to plow with it in the spring. He plays Pinochle,
5¢ a set and 10¢ a game and scratches his back and the side of his head a lot while
contemplating bids." That really didn't tell me all that much. Many boys had nice

smiles, drove old cars and played Pinochle in Strasburg and most played the accordion. After prodding on, mother said, "Don't you remember that awful lightening accident on that Mattern farm in 1935?" As an eight year old in 1935 I certainly did remember the tragedy.

Our prospective in-law, then 15, was mowing hay one summer Saturday afternoon in the same field his 14 year old brother was raking and his older sister and their father were hauling hay. The father was lifting hay to the sister who was stacking on the wagon. Just as their forks touched a bolt of lightening flashed from a thunder cloud and killed them both. The wagon was on fire and the horses ran off. The two brave little boys tamed the horses, unhitched them and ran for help.

At the wake, in their home, little two year old Myra walked from room to room calling her big sister.

Likable Al Mattern would spend his teen summers working on farms. Later he earned the Purple Heart in the Battle of the Bulge, bought a few tractors, become a prison guard in Bismarck, raised and college educated six contributing children, raised the card stakes and became an accomplished Bridge player - probably still scratching his head during bidding. Today he and my sister, Mary, spend summers in Bismarck and winter in Arizona.

* * * * *

KLEIN'S SUMMER KITCHEN

Joe Klein, my childhood playmate and school classmate and a Milwaukee, Wisconsin barber the past 50 years mailed this 1993 photo. The time worn, weatherbeaten, leaning, memory filled structure once served as the summer kitchen for Wendelin Kleins, just north of my Rosenthal church and just south of my Wells School #18. As a child I passed through Klein's farm on my way to school and played there many Sundays. Except for sleeping, the summer kitchen served as their living quarters during the summer.

Inside the ceiling and walls were of 1½ inch beaded pine. The gray painted floor had three inch wide tongue and groove fur boards. There was a wooden stand for the wash basin, soap and towel, and drinking pail with a dipper. The oil clothed dining table held a sugar jar and a jar with spoons and forks. A black, chrome framed cooking stove with a huge oven rested by the north wall. Mrs. Klein, my godmother, baked delicious round-the-loaf jelly bread in that oven. Pots and pans hung on the light green wall. By the stove rested a coal pail and an ash pail against which Mr. Klein cleaned his pipe. Summer breezes provoked the green pulldown shades, causing clicking sounds against the open windows. And there was always a cat or two roaming or eating from a dish on the floor and the ever present flies sometimes so thick we all took dish cloths and shooed them out the open door. There was laughter and kindness to me and lots of talk and good feeling in that summer kitchen and the sweet aroma of Mr. Klein's pipe.

But this tired old crumbler was not always a summer kitchen. It first was a schoolhouse before the more modern Wells School #18 was built, and stood just northeast of the new school. There it served pioneer children as they learned to speak, read and write in English. It doubled as a meeting place for early settlers and a voting precinct for men (before women could vote). As a schoolhouse its doors were never locked and it was always ready to shelter during prairie storms.

Though 100 years of 40 degrees below and 110 degrees above temperatures, rain, wind, hail, dust and snowstorms have ravaged its strength, this old schoolhouse summer kitchen basks in memories and refuses to go down.

* * * * *

CREAM STATIONS

A big cash crop for farmers in "My First World" was the cream their cows produced.

George Nold and Rochus Holzer ran cream stations in Strasburg. In Linton Jacob Rau and Linton Creamery bought cream. The creamery converted its product into ice cream and butter. The other buyers trucked and trained theirs to Oaks, Aberdeen, South Dakota, Valley City, Jamestown and Mandan. Farmers spent their weekly $3 to $5 checks at the grocery store and a little on gasoline for the weekly treks to town and church. When buying a car the criterion was, "is there room for a ten gallon cream can?"

But cream wasn't all these stations dealt in. Furbearing game and poultry were a big part of their business. Jackrabbits, swarming the prairies, were harvested by the wagon loads by farmers and sold to creameries for 15¢ a piece. Two boxes of 50 .22 short rifle shells cost about 25¢. Weasels brought 75¢ and muskrats 50¢. Adult chickens went for 10¢ a pound, springers 42¢ a pound, turkeys were 14¢ and geese and ducks 25¢ a pound. Eggs brought 7¢ a dozen.

Hunting jackrabbits was not only a fun sport but profitable. The cream stations dumped them on ten foot mounds till there were enough, along with weasels and Beaver Creek muskrats to fill a train car. These furbearers were shipped to furries in St. Louis, Missouri. The carcasses ended up at fox and mink farms in Minnesota, Wisconsin and Iowa. The fur often returned to Linton and Strasburg via clothing salesmen as "Alaskan Fur" in the form of pink, green or brown coats and jackets for $75.

Cream stations often went farm to farm to buy live poultry. Chickens and turkeys roosted on the Schiermeister farm near "old town" in Linton till there were enough for a train car. They were fed and watered all the way to New York processing plants. These fresh poultry delights sold in the eastern gourmet eateries for porterhouse steak prices.   * * * * *

MY CRAB APPLE TREE

I've been tending my backyard crab apple tree for 39 years. It is both a mess and a joy. One day here I told it how I felt about the upcoming season.

80

As spring's floating clouds let in the warm sun and the gentle breeze bends your arms and fingers, you wake from your 39th winter nap holding the chickadee and goldfinch feeder on your arm. Sprouting leaves will soon appear from your appendages, first pale and then darker green. Your blossom buds will turn soft pink and bring humming bees by the hundreds. You will be mighty beautiful and have sweet fragrance, graduation pictures will be taken under your adorned branches.

But these blossoms you will soon shed and the wind will churn the little peddles and scatter them into rain gutters and sidewalks and bushes. They will wash into streets and clog sewers. Each blossom you will replace with a tiny green apple that will become a large marble sized fruit. Your leaves will grow thicker and darker green and you will provide shade and windbreak.

Soon your tired branches will stoop as the fruit becomes heavier by the day. The apples will redden and you will look very pretty, Christmas red and green. Your leaves will turn gorgeous golden and you will glean yellow on my fall oak staircase through the landing window. You will shed much of this attire and make the grass mushy and sticky and red and brown and wilty and ishy! But you will save some fruit for the winter cedar wax-wing.

In the warm fall sun your gooey fruit will lie red and plentiful on the once bright green grass. You will say, "Here is my contribution to reproduction." Then as I scoop your mess and haul it to the garbage you will again say, "Are these worth no more?" To that I will say, "I thank you for the beauty, shade, windbreak and children climbing you gave all summer. I clear this away now to make you look less wasteful. But I know next spring you will do this all over again, you crab apple tree!"

* * * * *

THE LUCKY ONES

After reading the book, "*I Hope, Reminiscences and Reflections of Raisa Gorbachev*", Baisa's story of bad times in Russia after 1905, I sent her a copy of "*My First World*". My story of my Germans from Russia who fled Russia from 1889-1910 and settled in Strasburg. She will immediately realize the fortune of these emigrants, no matter what hardships they endured early on in America.

Raisa was born in 1932 in Siberia. Her father's birthplace in 1907 was in Ukrainia. He moved to Siberia in 1929 to work on railroads. Raisa describes frequent moves and living in shacks. Her peasant mother lived in a labor camp in Siberia. She plowed, seeded and harvested the fields, milked cows and raised six children. Her grandfather was visited during the night by soldiers and taken away without a trace. She called this the purge of the 1930's. The purge destroyed all churches and schools, murdered suspected "disloyal" peasants and forever separated families. Although Raisa never mentioned the names of Lenin Trotsky and Stalin, these mad rulers who fought for power, wars and civic wars, and how Trotsky had to flee the country and was hunted down in Mexico and killed by Stalin with a pick ax, she did tell of the war with Germany, constant fear and displacement of people.

Because her father worked for the government on the railroad, Raisa got to go to school and was chosen to attend the University of Moscow in 1949. She tells of the sparse conditions on the train to the university and how fortunate she was to be chosen.

Today, one hundred years after the Strasburg immigrants, peasants in Russia have not progressed one iota. Broad faced and solemn women in babushkas are milking cows at communal farms. Our German Russian relatives are being shipped to Poland and Germany by the thousands. Before the purge our Strasburg people communicated with relatives in the old country, sent pictures of North Dakota homesteads and sod houses. Recent visitors to the homeland were shown such pictures these Russians still carry with them.

Yes, we are the lucky ones.

* * * * *

ELECTION DAY

I witnessed a pleasurable day long event this past November 5th, election day. The Immanual United Church of Christ in Taylor sponsored a mega bake sale and craft show in the Opera House of this friendly rural Norwegian community. In charge was Jeanette Dohrmann who had invited me to show, sign and sell "*My First World.*" The Opera House has served the Taylor community since 1912 as the place for concerts, movies, dances, roller skating, meetings and its tall ceiling allows basketball events. The structure reminds me of the Blue Room in Strasburg, minus the lounge.

My booth occupied the space to the right of the entry way. Across from me ladies displayed, served and sold enormous quantities of pies, cakes, rolls, lefsa and numerous ethnic delicacies covering three long tables. From there crafts ringed the entire Opera House. Christmas green table cloths and red candles decked the many serving tables in the center. Coffeeing and enjoying pastries were the Bobbs, Dohrmanns, Ingets, Gjermundson, Haases, Hutchinsons, Larsens, Myrons, Marcusens, Naumanns, Paulsons, Ingvolds, Perhuses, Seversons, Jespersons, Vaagens and Booms after voting a few steps away in the City Hall. Sprinkled among these Norwegians were Germans from nearby Richardton who have tinged their blood with Foresters and Hoffs. There were no strangers. After 41 years of dental practice in Dickinson these pleasant faces were easily greeted. Not even a wet falling snow dampened the festive mood in Taylor that day.

As I left town in late afternoon I decided on a soda at the local coffee shop. The waitress asked me to take one and lay the change on the counter. Her friendly trusting self depicted the mood of the town. She was busy shaking 6-5-4 for the coffee with the regulars.

* * * * *

CHANGE AND PROGRESS

As we grow from children to teens, attend schools and mature into young men and women we become confident in chosen occupations. We just know from what we've learned that we are at a super level to begin our life's work. We know the latest and are equal to anyone in our field.

This attitude continues and at first occupational refresher courses are taught by people older than we are. Suddenly these presenters are younger, and later yet, half our age. Personal adjustment to this age spread can be challenging and difficult.

All of a sudden we realize that school should have taught us to be a constant student and to always welcome and enjoy change, that new concepts and new people lead to progress and growth.

Shirley experienced this change when after the children were grown, she turned to nursing again. Her refresher mentors and peers were half her age. Attitude and desire to conquer new methods and gain knowledge soon took precedence, resulting in interesting satisfying employment with Home Health Care, a field of nursing nonexistent in 1955 when she entered nursing.

In my three times weekly, journalism classes at Dickinson State University, Professor Robbins, fortyish, announces, "Your writings are to be on discs except for Ed Keller who is not yet in the 20th century, he may type his, no long hand, Ed, please". Do I need to take a computer class next semester to stay with these exciting young people? After all, I am dealing here with a double generation gap. In a chronological sense I could be father to the teacher and grandfather to the students.

I asked Dr. David Solheim, Language Chair at the University about his feelings the first time he encountered a younger teacher. He said "that the pursuit of knowledge knows not age, race, creed, or sex. I feel comfortable in these college classes."

I also admire more and more the young dentists that teach me at refresher courses. Over the years they have taught me theories, methods and dental materials not thought of 40 years ago. I feel comfortable and fortunate to study from and among them---so I can keep on keeping on.

* * * * *

WRITING A STORY

Many of you remember Father Samuel Homsey, a Precious Blood priest, who served at Sacred Heart Church in Rosenthal and at St. Anthony's Church in Linton in the 1960's and 1970's. I remember him as my high school English teacher at Canton, Ohio in 1941 and 1942. Both of us remember him as a hard taskmaster. In his determination to teach writing Fr. Homsey required us students to write for the first five minutes of every class. We chose our own subject. "But I don't know what to write about today," came complaints. "Then get busy and write about that," Homsey advised. The persistent priest never took "no" for an answer - and we wrote and wrote. Writing is a matter of starting and never quitting he'd say. Let your mind drift and explore ideas and experiences was his counsel.

Along with subject matter writing requires good grammar, focus, polish and creating complications and resolutions. For many years I never saw a book that could tell how to write. Recently I came upon a book, "*Writing for Story*" by Jon Franklin that does tell step by step how to write a story. Franklin portrays his craft secrets in two of his Pulitzer Prize short stories in a simple understandable fashion that would make Father Samuel Homsey smile. The book would be on Homsey's required reading list.

Since writing is a creative art it is therapeutic for the writer and hopefully entertaining for the reader. Years ago I threw away my writings after they had accomplished the former. Today I have more time and so try to add more focus and polish in order to produce the latter.

And, oh yes, the persistence Father Samuel Homsey demonstrated remains, especially to get writings published. Then it is ten times more fun.

* * * * *

"HOW'S RETIREMENT, DOC?"

Since the October 15th, 1996 retirement from dental practice, that question from friends and ex-dental patients is a daily given.

Well its delightful, leisurely and thoroughly enjoyable, like a deharnessed horse, rolling in the ground. Not since the age of five have I had more freedom from school and work. There are six Saturdays in my week.

The ultimate pleasure is to write and read when there is feeling for it, rather than when there is time for it. I love to compose, review and re-write these mini essays I use for columns. My intention is to publish another book containing them.

Schools are extending invitations for me to read "*My First World*" to North Dakota History classes. The fine details of how a small area of North Dakota was settled, told by one who lived it, intrigues students. I am also presenting to school science classes the connection of dentistry to science. Students find fluorides, bonding, implants and all aspects of dental science extremely relevant.

Science groups in my area and around the state are having me read to them from "*My First World*". These pioneers experience memories, laughter, tears and good feeling in between.

There is daily mail correspondence, answering inquiries, sending books, marketing newspapers around the country, and the ever present telephone. Future writing with unforeseen opportunities lurk. They are good fortunes and privileges, that keep one on the problem solving side of life.

* * * * *

SHAF DICH NAUS

When I was a little boy, four to seven years old, on my Emmons County farm, and didn't have a job yet, and wandered idly around the house, mother would say "Shaf dich naus, und kom nit rein bis essa zeit." (Get outside and don't come in till eating time). Outside there was the barn, chicken coop, straw barn, car shed and smoke house to wander in and out of. There were the chickens and pigs to see and talk to and some birds. I especially looked forward to seeing my father and brothers coming from the fields with the work horses.

But I had a play farm of my very own, my own wheat and oats and corn fields, fenced in with wood pegs and binder twine. I worked my little farm with toy horses (clothes pins with string around the heads), five to a plow, four to a seed drill, two to a cultivator and two to a wagon. Irrigation from the horse tank assured a crop, even in dry years, and my confidence abounded.

When the winter cold prevented me from sledding and skating on the dam, mother said, "Shat dich nuf," "nuf" was the attic bedroom with the corn straw mattresses. There in my sheepskin coat, I made toy sleds from empty farmer match boxes or scraped frost from peek-through nails on the roof boards, or played with my brother's accordion, or cleared up tiny piles that drained from the 100 pound flour sacks stored there . . . after mice chewed holes during the night.

Today, 66 years later, I again don't have a job. Mother's "Shaf dich naus" and "Shaf dich nuf" taught creativity beyond her realization.

* * * * *

WISCONSIN VACATION

Your editor, Allan Burke, has invited me to pursue my writing hobby in your newspaper, the *Emmons County Record*. Since I was reared in Emmons County, the *Record* is the first newspaper I ever saw and just hearing the name causes a warm feeling for me.

My first writings will contain past and present experiences as I venture through life. They will be candid and reader friendly. I hope they will prove useful and entertaining.

As this summer comes to an end I will tell you abut the high point of my 1995 summer. Shirley is the youngest of 10 children and she is 62 years old. The other nine children all gathered with us over the Fourth of July weekend at Shafer's Resort in Crivitz, Wisconsin. Shafer's Resort was established by John Shafer, an immigrant from Germany after World War II. Shafer bought a farm on the Peshtigo River, started serving restaurant meals from his farm house, built a supper club and a motel. His supper club specializes in chicken, fish and white potatoes. He raises his own potatoes in a 20 acre field every year.

In addition to the 10 Maloney siblings 33 of their 36 children were also present in Crivitz with their spouses and children. There were 150 people, ages three weeks to

84 years, from 11 states, Florida, Louisiana, Tennessee, Oregon, California, Arizona, North Dakota, Minnesota, Wisconsin, Michigan and Pennsylvania.

For much of the week we occupied most all of the facilities at the resort. Shafer's is equipped with playgrounds, outdoor heated swimming pool, bonfire pit with logs for nocturnal songs and suds, river boating, water skiing and fishing, a golf course at walking distance, gazebos and picnic tables among the tall trees and over fifty motel rooms with kitchenettes. We were blessed with beautiful Wisconsin weather and all suppers were picnic style. This event happened to coincide with Shirley's and my 40th wedding anniversary.

If any of you young readers are interested in doing something like this 40 years from now, attend Marquette University in Milwaukee, Wisconsin; meet a student nurse from Marinette, Wisconsin in your sophomore year; don't let her out of your sight for two years; marry her; come back to North Dakota; raise a family and then all return to Crivitz, Wisconsin, over the Fourth of July week in the year 2035. It will be an almost overwhelming pleasure for that nurse to be in the presence of all her children and grandchildren plus all of her siblings at the same time . . . especially if she spent two years planning and coordinating the event.

Editor's Note: We welcome Dr. Edward Keller as a columnist and contributor this week. He was recently featured in the *Record* for publishing a book about growing up in Emmons County, "*My First World*".

* * * * *

PRAIRIE MIRACLE

In "My First World" 1932-33 my father engineered a dam on a large gully that lead through our farm. The watercourse carried cloud bursts and snow melts on their way to Beaver Creek, two miles beyond.

During the two summers and two falls, between field work, tons and tons of earth from the gully and the future spillway became the 100 yard long, 40 foot high and 30 foot wide dike. Neighbors with four-horse scrappers helped my father build his dream. There were John and Tony Hagel, Wendelin Klein, Mike Wolf, Adam Bossert, Andy Kraft, John Lauinger and more. I loved to bring them water and sandwiches and run barefoot in the cool loose damp fresh earth, watching the mounting pile become the dike.

The bottom row of rocks (boulders) that ribbed the dike needed five horses each to be dragged into place from nearby prairie hills and rock piles. Wagon loads of rocks piled on top of these boulders protected the dike from lapping water.

When full the dam reached 100 yards across and backed up water over 300 yards. This miracle on the prairie became a swimming oasis for all the neighbors, the Krafts, Hagels, Kleins, Schwabs, Jahners, Wolfs, Lauingers, Bosserts, Wickenheisers, and more. My father bought a paddle boat from the Dietrich blacksmith shop in Strasburg, a floating diving platform and fun rowing. Adults dived from the dike.

Livestock drank and waded leisurely on hot sunny days. Waterfowl nested there. My uncle and godfather, Frank Glatt from Burnstad, never visited without his shotgun. I skipped rocks on the water and played with turtles and frogs and little snakes and watched my dog fetch rubber balls. I rode my pony as he swam the width (smoother than any ride since). Mother's lush garden grew nearby. During the winter I skated and sledded as did my neighbors. My father harvested ice into an earthen cellar for summer butter and cream cooling and, of course, ice cream.

One day Emmons County Agent, Ben Barrett, took a picture of my father by the boat dock and it appeared in the *Emmons County Record*.

* * * * *

INSECT FRIENDS

I recently learned some facts of our everyday warm weather insect friends. Ruthie Unruh presented this information to her students at Jefferson Grade School in Dickinson. I summarized it and will share it with you.

Fleas can jump eight inches into the air, about 100 times their height. They are difficult to kill because they have no neck, no waist and no wings. Their bodies are covered in armour plates.

Fleas are born full grown. They can beat their wings more than 10,000 beats a minute. On short flights they can travel 50 miles an hour.

Male mosquitoes are harmless. Only female mosquitoes are after your blood. They need blood to boost egg production. Also it is only the female mosquito that buzzes.

Ants find their way back to their hills by leaving chemical trails. They run a short way, stop, press their bodies to the ground and leave a spot of chemical. Ants can carry 50 times their weight. They eat anything as long as it is juicy. When they take solid food into their mouths they squeeze for the juice and spit out the rest.

Only adult male crickets chirp. Females have ears on their knees and just listen. Chirping crickets can tell the temperature. Just count the chirps in 15 seconds. Then add 40 to the number and this will give you a degree in fahrenheit with surprising accuracy.

Butterflies weigh as much as two rose petals and fly thousands of miles each year.

Grasshoppers are so nutritious that pound for pound they are three times as nutritious as red meat.

The female moth produces a scent that a male moth can smell a mile away.

If you ever see an insect that is yellow, red or black, stay away. Insects with these colors are often poisonous.　　　* * * * *

GREAT CONTEMPORARIES

Some of America's greatest inventors and industrial giants of the past are Thomas Edison, 1841-1947, Harvey Firestone, 1868-1938, Alexis Carrol, 1837-1944 and Charles Lindberg, 1902-1977. All five men not only lived about the same time but shared each others friendship and worked together on projects.

Edison holds 1,093 patents ranging from the light bulb, movie camera and phonograph to synthetic rubber. At his death he was pondering harnessing the wind and the sun to preserve natural resources. Once asked what he thought to be the greatest invention he answered, "the mind of a child."

A thinker, he liked to go fishing without bait, to be totally left alone. At a science convention Edison met a young Henry Ford. At the time Edison was interested in inventing an electric car. Ford was working on a motorized buggy in his back yard. Pleased by Ford's idea Edison said to him, "Young man that is the thing. Your car is self contained, no boiler, no battery, no smoke or steam. Keep at it." Edison was Ford's boyhood idol and the car Ford invented became the future General Motor Car Company. He left that company to build a cheaper type car for the working man and formed the Ford Motor Company. Ford gave Edison the first of each subsequent model; the Model T, Model A, V-8 and Lincoln. At the time of his death Henry Ford was pondering a car made from organic sources.

While working for a buggy factory Harvey Firestone invented rubber tires. Henry Ford contacted him for tires for his car. Firestone had just founded a new pneumatic air tire and convinced Ford to try them. Ford ordered thousands of tires from Firestone. So they contacted inventor Edison and encouraged him to invent synthetic rubber, which he did, from the goldenrod plant. Firestone founded hundreds of car accessory stores throughout the United States.

Charles Lindberg, the father of aviation, shrunk the world with his historic transatlantic flight. He helped Ford build war plane engines for World War II. As a civilian test pilot he flew 50 combat missions in the South Pacific. After the war he started airline service. But the destructive power of the airplane during the war soured him on airplanes and he spent the rest of his life on planet conservation around the world.

Dr. Alexis Carrol became the father of modern surgery. He discovered methods to treat wounds in both world wars. Carrol earned the Nobel Prize for his work on successful blood vessel surgery. Charles Lindberg invented a purfusion pump with Carrol that helped tissue to survive away from their organs.

These five men invented the twentieth century and transformed our lives. They were most creative and foresighted, all had the desire to preserve dwindling natural resources.

* * * * *

BY ASSOCIATION

At. St. Joseph's Academy and College, Collegeville, Indiana, where I attended my senior year of high school, seniors resided at Gaspar Hall with college freshman and sophomores, senior privilege, they called it. Our voices had turned bass and we were shaving regularly among the acne. As seniors we were permitted to smoke tobacco.

It was 1944 and war rations were in effect. Camels and Lucky Strikes went to the troops, but Brother Dave, the school procurator, usually managed a few cartons of Raleighs for us. To prove our manhood and growing independence we filled the recreation room with thick blue clouds of smoke. It was sickening. My throat would collapse at first inhale attempts. Eyes watered and burned and the stomach churned. But I was a man. I lit fag after fag and my body kept revolting.

After Thanksgiving the recreation room phonograph often played a popular new song, "*White Christmas*", sung by a young crooner, Bing Crosby.

I saw him play the role of a priest in a movie called "*The Bells of St. Mary's*". He looked like my Latin teacher.

Since 1944 every Christmas season brings "*White Christmas*" and with it reminders of the recreation room, blue smoke and the actual stomach churning that made me a man.

* * * * *

BOOK SIGNING

On Saturday, December 2nd, 1995, Shirley and I visited, "My First World" country in Linton and Strasburg. We showed the book at the Pin Place in Strasburg from 10 a.m. to 1 p.m. and at Linton Drug from 2 p.m. to 4 p.m. The friendly faces of old time acquaintances and relatives were refreshing and memories abounded.

In Strasburg there was my brother, Debert, and his wife, Alice, the cheerful personality of Al Dosch, the sparkling eyes of Jimmy Schwab, the pleasant demeanor of Ed Vander Vorst and Katie and Al Kramer. Katie is one of Carl Keller's 18 children. Al is a former altar boy buddy of mine at Rosenthal church. I can still focus Al in his thick curly hair with his red cassock and white surplice we all wore serving Mass in the 1930's. Katie Wald was there too and she showed me three of the books she has written about the Hague area. Matty Lipp, the town postmaster graced our time. Before we left the Pin Palace treated us all with wonderful chicken and rice soup. It was an enjoyable three hours in Strasburg and thanks to all the many other friendly people we visited with there.

After we moved up to Linton we had another bowl of soup, borscht, at Mr. J's. Then we drove to Seeman Park for a little snooze in our reclining car seats and enjoyed the windless, cloudless 60° sun through the car windows. At Linton Drug, Toni, Bernice and pharmacist, Tommy Fischer welcomed Shirley and me with a table, coffee and chocolates. We enjoyed visiting with Martin Scherr's friendly, interested personality. Reverend Arvin and Augusta (Nieuwsma) Roos had missed us in Strasburg but paid a wonderful visit in Linton. Arvin liked the brochures and took with him an ample supply.

Smiling Theresa Bosch Stoppler spent time with us too. Her devotion to Rosenthal Church memories is one of extreme reverence. We met Dawn Senger. She and her husband own the Vetter and Klein farms and farm the Hagel land too. Mrs. Horner, an heir of Wendelin Horner of Rosenthal paid us a nice visit with sentimental comments. Lorraine Tschritter, a clerk at the Willow's Store was a welcome visitor. She found her late husband, Danny, listed among the 1940 Emmons County 8th grade graduates listed in the book. Elizabeth Kelsch Schmidt, also a clerk at Willow's Store had many things to reminisce because we had both attended Wells School. Bartender, Marcella Keller at the Happy Hour was a classmate of my sister, Eleanor and asked of her where abouts. We also met Marilyn Haak, the friendly activities director from the Strasburg Nursing Home. She told us how much the residents at the nursing home are enjoying a copy of "*My First World*" I had sent them.

Thanks Pin Place and Linton Drug for your wonderful hospitality. As we left "My First World" country I felt happy that the book has warmed many hearts.

* * * * *

TERRENCE KARDONG

Terrence Kardong is a monk at Benedictine Abbey in Richardton. But this doesn't qualify him for any special distinction because there are many monks at the Abbey. They all perform routine monk "things" like assembling in church cubicles before sunrise and chanting prayers till daylight, working the soil, earning PhDs in universities over the world and return to tend cattle or kitchens or print shops, or do parish work or teach at the University of Mary.

What ascends Terrence from the pack is an enormous talent as a writer. His subtle humor is sprinkled into most of his paragraphs, poking fun at himself and his fellow monks. He often employs not-so-often used works like "vitiate or forfend" that engage a readers' dictionary.

Among his literary charges is the editorialship of a quarterly newsletter to friends of the Abbey. The format in this well organized, flowery, artistically created and highly entertaining writing features a story plus a month by month chronicle of Abbey happenings, visitors and monk "things". Pictures appear. This October's issue presented the old 1950, no longer in use, school buildings being demolished, a PhD monk busy at the print shop, and two stout, bearded monks in sandals and untucked shirts headworking Socrates at a community picnic.

Usually I enjoy this writing for style and literary entertainment alone. Terrance can create humor and action in something as simple as paint drying or grass growing. In this issue however, the content of the story surpasses the style. Terrence engages the topic of Work and Prayer as it relates to a monk and to a lay person. Is work prayer or is prayer work? He tells that his hero, Benedict, said a monastic day should be three hours of church, five hours of work and three hours of biblical study. Terrence said, "because it takes time and energy to pursue a monastic existence, this becomes very difficult if one's work uses up all that energy". He readily sees a conflict here when administrators of modern institutions have slots to fill.

The story is provocative and exciting. Terrence covers an area from workaholics to work interfering with the business of being a monk. However he admits that for the sake of survival some monks may tip the tripod of Benedict in favor of work. You could conclude from reading this story that Terrence is not marketing monks to the secular labor force. It also makes one understand why a PhD monk does garden or kitchen duties since work is only a fraction of his main job which is to be a monk. The story is totally enlightening to the lay population. For 32¢ you can be on Terrence's list of friends.

* * * * *

SCHOOL JOBS

In the summer of 1949 during my St. Thomas College years in St. Paul, jobs for some reason were scarce. The want ads served as my "Job Service". There I discovered a door to door sales opportunity that promised an irresistible value to the fortunate persons who answered the bell. For 75¢ down and 50¢ a month the postman would deliver the *Saturday Evening Post* plus a free subscription to the *Ladies Home Journal*. The 75¢ was my commission. I learned much about who lives in apartments, bungalows and river road mansions in St. Paul. Out of about 150 calls a day twenty would be sales.

The summer of 1952 found me at Marquette University in Milwaukee, Wisconsin. The breweries were on strike. Another job problem arose, but armed with previous sales experience I again hit the streets. This time the ads led me to an absolutely runner-free nylon stocking, just new on the market, sold only door to door at $1.50 a pair, three pair to a package and 50% commission. As the doors opened the occupants seemed surprised at a runnerless nylon stocking. They seemed entertained watching my demonstration. With the foot part of the stocking tied on the door knob I put my hand inside the hose and ran my fingernails up and down.

99

"Unheard of," they would say, "by now there should be five runs." I had a great product and fairly smooth fingernails. Factory jobs always paid well and in August of that summer the Allis Chalmer Manufacturing Co. hired me for foundry work. For the remainder of the summer I casted steel bomb shells to blow up North Korea.

A good Saturday and one-night-a-week job was selling shoes for the Brower Shoe Co. in Milwaukee, Wisconsin. Brower's was a children's shoe store and carried Stride-Rites, a good quality leather soled shoe, both ties and straps selling for as high as $12 a pair. The store had a state of the art fluoroscope on which customers stood to determine the fit. Customers took numbers as they entered the store and waited their turn. My commission was 9% and I once had a $300 sales day.

Breweries were the best paying jobs. I supplied cans and bottles to filling lines or loaded cases and cases onto railroad cars for North Dakota, Montana and anywhere for $2.75 an hour, time and half for overtime, of which there was plenty.

* * * * *

MY EARLIEST MUSICAL SOUNDS

As a little German Russian child in "My First World" time, at my Strasburg farm, I was exposed to four kinds of music.

Accordion sounds of waltzes and polkas permeated all house parties and dance halls. They were the same ethnic musical notes heard on the train from Odessa, Russia to Hamberg, Germany; on the boat to Ellis Island, New York; on the train to Aberdeen, South Dakota and on the ox carts to Strasburg. Accordion music was cheerful, smile

100

provoking, spirited and toe tapping. There was an abundance of accordion players in Strasburg.

There was the cowboy singing guitar music on the radio waves from the Carter Family. My 7th and 8th grade strumming teacher, Ehli Cruschwutz taught me "*Cowboy Jack*".

My father acquired records of John Phillip Sousa's band marches. I played them on the victrola. The Linton City Band was my favorite event during Fourth of July celebrations at Seeman Park in Linton. At the band stand I became engrossed by the snappy, fast moving, exciting marches, pushed by the drums and cymbals.

Rosenthal Church featured the pump organ. Ignatz Kuhn, Tony Hagel and Fred Bosch reverently intoned "*The High Mass Of The Angels*", "*Schtile, Nachg Heilige Nacht*", "*O Groser Gott*" and two benediction songs.

After leaving "My First World" my high school music teacher, Father Luktemeyer, taught me to play violin for his orchestra. He played records of William Tell and other classicals and narrated stories behind the musical compositions, and I was fascinated. I learned to play the tuba for the band. Band music at high school and college sports events consisted of all marches and "*The Star Spangled Banner*".

As time passed, swing band music, new country western and more came to my attention. I liked all the music I was exposed to except rock music. There I had a conflict concerning loudness, melody, harmony and lyrics. But my first four kinds of music from my childhood left an indelible impression in my heart. It didn't matter how long I was away from them, the minute I heard them my face became a smile, or my toes

began to tap, or both.   * * * * *

NAME CHANGE

Ismay, Montana changed its name to Joe and reaped instant publicity and fame.

Located on a gravel road off of U.S. Highway #12, south of Glendive and twenty miles

northwest of Baker, Ismay had gotten its name in 1910 from a railroad magnate who had

two daughters, Isabel and May. In 1912 its citizens nearly discarded the name after

Bruce Ismay chairman of the shipping line on the sinking Titanic, allegedly elbowed

ahead of women and children to lifeboats.

When in 1993 Kansas City Chiefs of the National Football League acquired the

famous quarterback, Joe Montana, a Kansas City disc jockey invented the idea to rename

a Montana town, Joe. After receiving turndowns from such towns, as Molt, Iron, Straw,

Yaak, Slumptown and Crackerville, Ismay, population 28, consented to change its name

to Joe. Instant fame transformed the town. Signs indicating former businesses, Robert

Livery, Grey Gables Hotel, Ryan Clothing-Millinery and Maternity, Cass-Hamilton

Store, J.E. Prindle Real Estate, and Brackett Hotel sprang up on the former sights. The

south wall of the Catholic church read in big red letters: Joe's Career . . . Notre Dame

1975-78 . . . National Champs 1977, San Francisco 1978-93 . . . 4 Super Bowls . . . Joe

3 MVP's, Kansas City Chiefs.

National media exploded with the news. *Sports Illustrated, The Wall Street

Journal, New York Times,* and *USA Today* all featured Joe, Montana. All 28 citizens

attended a Chief's game and had an audience with Joe Montana. A San Francisco TV station shot and showed footage of the town. The first Joe, Montana Day was celebrated July 3rd, 1993 with a parade, rodeo, cowboy poetry, Ismay school reunion, fiddlers' jamboree, dance and fireworks. Retired couples in Winnebagos and tourists by the thousands swelled the area. The event drew three to four thousand tourists and filled motels the 200 miles to Billings, Montana.

July 5th, 1997, featured the fifth Joe, Montana Day with a dance, hog roast, three on three basketball, beer gardens and all the fireworks. Although the crowds have waned from past years, local postmistress of Joe, Montana 59336, Loreen Nemits, said Joe, Montana Day will continue every 4th of July until Joe Montana's name is in the National Football Hall of Fame in Canton, Ohio.

Joe, Montana, zip code 59336, sports a new fire hall and community center where T-shirts, jackets, sweatshirts, bumper stickers, baseball caps, coffee mugs, cards and letters franked Joe, Montana are sold. Once the remains of times gone by, Ismay - Joe, Montana is now a museum and a national tourist town.

* * * * *

excerpts from

"My First World"

MY SACRED HEART CHURCH

At Rosenthal different musical people served as organists. Ignatius Kuhn, Ignatz Bosch and Tony Hagel played the organ and led the choir during my years there. These men also led the Rosary before Mass and taught Catechism during summer school at Wells #18 for a three week summer session. Catechism school was a fun time. All the children from the church attended regardless of what school they attended during regular school term. There was a summer atmosphere and Beaver Creek was again our playground. After the March school dismissal the floors, desks and walls of the school were varnished. I enjoyed the fresh varnish scent during the summer. This school session was conducted in the German language, a reversal from regular school. There was no fear of punishment for being caught speaking German on school grounds.

Sacred Heart Church was a mission of St. Aloysius, also a farm church, nine miles to the east. The priest resided at St. Aloysius. In 1921 the Diocese of Bismarck contracted with the Precious Blood Community of Religion in Ohio to supply priests for about ten parishes. These parishes included St. Aloysius, Rosenthal, Linton, Hazelton, Hebron, Grassy Butte, Fayette, Killdeer, Hazen and Dodge. These priests remained in our Diocese until July 1993. I had the great fortune of being educated in their Ohio high school and college after 1941. Precious Blood priests were the only kind of priests I ever knew until I was nineteen years old. The first priest I remember at Rosenthal was Father Henry Friedel. He was a small man with an even temper and a great love for North Dakota. He was well loved by everybody he came in contact with. Father Friedel baptized me, served me First Holy Communion, I took Henry for my Confirmation name, and he taught me to serve Mass. Father Friedel left me with fond memories of priests. During snowy winters priests were brought the nine miles to Rosenthal in a horse drawn sled by a farmer from St. Aloysius. Poor roads and snow did not permit any cars in farm areas during the winter season. But only the worst of the blizzards kept the people in "My First World" from church on Sundays. If the priest could not be present there was the Rosary and other prayers led by the organist and Catechism class to round out the ceremonies.

The second priest I remember was Father Denzal, an Ohio acclimated man, who did not like North Dakota drought and hard times. He was clearly not meant to be in North Dakota. Some of his sermons were spirited. The times were economically bad with money in short supply. My father was in charge of collections and many Sundays the entire take was under two dollars. During one sermon Father Denzal gave he said, "Ich kan nicht leben von luft und sunshein," which means, "I can't live on air and sunshine." However, Father Denzal did receive many chickens, pork and potatoes from farmers. He spent only a couple years in North Dakota. The next priest was a big Wisconsin farm boy named Father Charles Meyer. With that good Ohio Seminary training of work and endurance, he filled the bill for Dakota life. The drought was beginning to lift and he pitched header boxes for his parishioners during harvest. In those days a priest was a very respected person. Whenever he entered among his flock everyone rose to their feet. He was addressed in the "polite" form of the German language; the one saved for rulers, judges and aged grandmothers.

Priests were the only educated people that there were in "My First World" on a regular basis. My father once told me that a being a priest was the highest honor one could ever achieve. He said a priest has an education, respect and a nice living. The seminaries themselves taught that the highest vocation on earth is the priesthood. Then came the health profession, next the teaching profession. The thinking was soul, body and mind. "My First World" people turned to their priest for advice for almost every facet of their lives and generally accepted it. Priests had enormous power over their parishioners. People needed their permission to do manual work on Sundays and Holy Days, even during harvest. They performed his wishes out of respect for the priesthood and the Catholic Church, and out of fear of eternal consequences. Some decisions were made to avoid the wrath of the confessional.

* * * * *

ENTERTAINMENT

The John Schwab farm was south of Lauingers. John and his wife Magdalina had ten offspring: Joe, Larry, John, Jimmy, Florence, Irene, LaVern, Clarence, Antonia and Clara. John Schwab, Sr. was the most accomplished accordion player around. He had many students who would stay at his home while he instructed them. Lawrence Welk was an accordion buddy of John Schwab's and they enjoyed many a "jam session" together.

Strasburg was synonymous with accordion music. No one read music notes, all the waltzes and polkas were played by ear. Schwab was the most in demand and commanded the largest fee for a dance night, $5.00. He could play his instrument so loud one could hear him from the Blue Room the minute you crossed the railroad tracks into Strasburg. Many accordion players like Anton Hagel with his brother, John, on the clarinet, Matt and Pete Schwab, Tony Bauman, Mike Dosch and the Mastel brothers played for dances on Name's Days or at most any celebration at peoples' homes.

Name's Days were very popular during the winter season. If your name was Frank, your Name's Day was on the Feast of St. Francis, December 3rd. That was my father's Name's Day. Many people came to our house on that evening. My mother prepared food for days prior. It was fun and many German songs were sung. The women sat in one room and the men in another. It always sounded like everyone was talking at the same time, and loud. At times there was an accordion player and dancing. A chair on the kitchen table was his stage and the rest of the house was the dance floor.

There was a radio station in Mandan, KGCU, over which various old time orchestras played thirty minute segments once or twice a week. Listeners sent in requests to have music dedicated to each other. Aspiring musicians listened and learned from these radio waves. Charlie Richter and Thomas Gutenburg were two of these radio accordionists. Sam and his City Slickers was another musical treat over KGCU featuring Emil Dockter on the accordion. Their theme song was the *"Clarinet Polka"*. People did farm chores early to free up time to be in the house for these popular melodies. It was happy entertainment.

Another radio music show came over station WNAX in Yankton, South Dakota. It was Lawrence Welk's famous music. From a radio station in far off Texas came the harmonizing voices and guitar playing of the Carter Family. Their theme song was,

"Keep on the sunny side of life. It will help you every day, it will brighten all your way, so keep on the sunny side of life!"

Popular radio shows were the Jack Benny Show, Amos and Andy, Popeye the Sailorman, Ma Perkins and of course, all the Joe Lewis fights. Lewis was everybody's hero in the 1930's. His heavyweight fights with Max Bear, Gene Tunny, Buddy Bear and even Charlie Retsolf from Ellendale were the talk before and after church in Rosenthal . Retsolf took his money from the fight and bought a farm in the Red River Valley. You didn't dare turn on the radio even two minutes late for fear of missing the fight. That's how fast Lewis knocked people out.

Tony Hagel made and sold crystal radio sets, ear phones and all, for $3.00. Speaker radios came in various sizes and were powered by batteries.

* * * * *

WELLS SCHOOL #18

Wells School was a happy experience for me. It was there that I learned how to speak elementary English and to read. I loved my school. The farm school term was from September through March. Children were needed for spring planting, so April and May were not school months.

The school grounds contained the school, a barn for horses and an outdoor plumbing building, one side marked "Boys" and the other marked "Girls". The inside of the school consisted of two walls with windows and two walls with blackboards. A rack of Randy McNally maps, the framed Ten Commandments, a picture of the President of the United States at the time, a picture of Franklin D. Roosevelt and a picture of the

First Father of our Country, George Washington, graced the tops of the blackboards. The library was a world globe, a large dictionary and a set of encyclopedias in the back corner. Rows of desks faced the teacher's large desk in the front of the room. A pot-bellied stove in the middle-back part of the room was our comforter as its' sides became red hot at 30° below zero in the winter.

President Roosevelt was our "economic savior" and was revered by everyone. There was a time when I thought he had authored the Ten Commandments hanging on the wall next to his picture. All we needed to do was look in our lunch pail to see his apples and oranges.

Of all the United States Presidents in office during my lifetime, President Franklin D. Roosevelt was the dearest to my heart. I was playing softball at about 3:30 p.m., April 12th, 1945, during my senior year of high school when I heard of his death. The news left me with a heavy heart as I recalled his care of us in the 1930's. I remember the slogan when he ran for a fourth term and Truman was his vice-presidential candidate, "Be Human, Vote for Roosevelt and Truman."

Roosevelt was the author of the GI Bill of Rights during World War II which later paid for almost all of my college education after my military service. Of interest here is that the other big education bill in the history of America, The Land Grant College Act, came after another war---the Civil War. It set aside land for colleges, that is North Dakota State University. The schools received food commodities to be prepared at school. Theresa Bosch, was the school cook, The NYA program hired her. She was the most creative with the pot-bellied stove. She soaked dried peas overnight, stewed prunes and heated up canned meat. She brought her own water when there wasn't any snow to melt because the school did not have a water well. The school prepared lunches were fun and good. School lunches during the years when Theresa didn't cook were often syrup sandwiches in gallon pails and an apple. Syrup mixed with peanut butter was a tasty sandwich spread.

Well School #18 was located on Beaver Creek. I always wished I could have lived on Beaver Creek. We played there often during our school freetime. It was one big playground. The water, trees and bushes were settled with rabbits, snakes, pheasants, prairie chickens, turtles with fish and crabs under the rocks. The bushes and trees bore berries, cherries, plums and chestnuts. There were flowers and cactus. Different earth formations were exciting "Hide and Seek" sites. We skated on the ice. We harvested little Y-shaped branches for sling shots and larger branches to make stilts.

* * * * *

HORSE PETS

Often times, cattle and horses would stray from herds. I thought it adventurous to ride from farm to farm on my pony, "Bessie," "Tricks" or "Pretty" for an entire day to inquire if anyone had seen a strange bull, cow or horse. It seemed to be quite a responsibility for an eleven or twelve year old. When I found the lost critter, the most fun was to cut it away from his new found friends and bring him home. My pony "Bessie" had an interesting history. My father bought her for $3 from my uncle, Burt Schneider, who lived in Fort Yates. It was illegal for Indian people to purchase alcoholic beverages. The story was that Uncle Burt traded something in a gallon jug for "Bessie".

111

This was most likely true because in later years, during World War II, Uncle Burt, who was then 40 years old, was caught in a similar act by the law. He had the option of going to jail or serving in the Army, he chose the latter. "Bessie" was a black mare with a white face and white socks. "Bessie" was gentle enough for even a baby to ride. She had a colt every year. "Tricks" was a brown Shetland pony. My father obtained him from the Ibachs, who lived east of Rosenthal parish, for a sack of left-over seed wheat and a heifer calf. "Tricks" was one fast little horse. In twelve minutes I could fetch mail a mile away, that included opening and closing a gate! Abusing pets was something my father frowned upon. A sweaty pony was a tell-tale sign of abuse but "Tricks" never sweat, lucky for me. He just didn't seem to have sweat glands. Christ Swoverland, the mailman from Strasburg seemed quite entertained when he met "Tricks" and me at the mailbox. Christ drove an ingenious vehicle during the winter months of his mail route. The rear wheels of his vehicle were caterpillar-like, the front end had both wheels and skis and he employed either as needed. Christ retired to Minneapolis. Years later, while going to school in St. Paul, I met him on a street car. The first thing he asked me was what happened to "Tricks". In regard to not abusing "Tricks" or any animal, my father had a practical way of controlling the number of pets I could have. I didn't know that cats had more than one litter until I was in Biology class in school. He always got to the barn first in the morning. He knew very well that overpopulation would lead to abuse and wasted milk if we had too many cats.

* * * * *

LINTON

Linton was my family's shopping and business town. I can describe the main street businesses as they were during the 1930's.

Upon entering Linton on the east side of Main Street, there was a football field on the right hand side. Fettig's Filling Station came next, right before the Linton Creamery. I liked the creamery for the wonderful chocolate malts they made. My mother liked it for the cream checks she got there to buy her weekly groceries.

Wilma's Bar and Bowling Alley came next. I used to set pins there for 5¢ a line. It was quite a trick to set the pins and scramble out of the pit in time to dodge the first bowling ball and scampering pins. Next came Sautter's, a cream buying station and then came Kremer's Hardware Store and Funeral Home. J.C. Penney was next, right before the Chevy garage. Martin's Shoe Repair, with the town's dentist, Dr. Edwin Mork, was after that.

Harry Lynn and Robert Chesrown were lawyers in the corner stone building. I knew them well because they bought many of the Indian artifacts and arrow heads I found on the dust-blown hills. Their walls were covered with framed arrowheads.

The bank occupied the other corner building with Bob's Bar and Bowling Alley next to it. Then came Schmaltz's Butcher shop and Grocery Store. Bauman's Ford Garage was next before the last business on the right side of Main, the "*Emmons County Record*". As we crossed the street there was Koeppen's Photo Shop. Jack and Jill's was a grocery store before Heyerman's Jewelry.

113

Petrie's was on the corner. Harry and Fred Petrie ran a huge department store with anything from needles to threshing machines, they said. One summer Petrie's offered a .22 single shot rifle for the family who brought in the most gopher tails by September. Gophers were swarming the county and damaging everything that did grow in the drought.

The Petrie family already had a very successful farming operation in Emmons County in 1888 when the first five scouts arrived from Russia. The scouts were very impressed with the Petrie farm.

A restaurant and bakery occupied the corner across from Petrie's. Then came the Post Office and Linton Drug, another place with good chocolate malts. The pharmacist was Paul McAllen. Hogue's Theater and Hotel came next followed by the Red Owl Store.

During my high school year in 1940 I saw some movies. The theatre, along with the regular movie and previews featured a newsreel, a serial and comics. The newsreel showed current events such as Hitler marching on Poland. The serial was "Fu Man Chu," continuous from week to week. Admission was 10¢.

After Red Owl, there was the Green Lantern Bar, the light plant, and then grain elevators and stockyards which finished out Main Street.

I loved to visit Linton with my parents. Some of the experiences that intrigued me most in my childhood in Linton were the treats in the creamery and the drug store, the neatly wrapped caramel candy at Petrie's, seven in a box for 1¢, the many cookie jars at Schmaltz's, the fruit and vegetables stacked so neatly in store windows, the enormous stacks of gloves, shirts and pants at Penny's, the new cars in the garages and the flush chain in the bathroom at Penny's. A real treat for me was to have lunch in town. Mr. Schmaltz sold bread and sausage and we lunched in his back room.

* * * * *

STRASBURG AND MORE

The dominant building feature of Strasburg is Saints Peter & Paul Catholic Church, called the "Cathedral of the Prairies." It is a stunning, beautiful work of art and today is on the National Register of Historic Sites. In the 1930's Strasburg was a vibrant town. As I entered from the east, the businesses on the right side began with the train depot and tracks. Next there was the Valentine Keller Implement and Hardware Store and Hotel. Valentine was my grandfather Mike's brother. The Miller Filling Station and Garage were next, then the Red and White Food Store, the Bank and Timmer's Beauty Salon, Schmaltz's Butcher Shop and Groceries followed. This was the same Schmaltz before he moved to Linton in 1937. A.J.'s Bar with upstairs dance hall was beside Schmaltz's. Schriner's Barbershop, Bauman Bowling and the Post Office followed. Bauman's Theater was last with Schumacher Ford Garage just to the north of it. Crossing Main Street to go back east there was a harness and shoe shop. Klein's General Store came before a cream station, then Kraft Brothers Clothing and Food and City Hall. Next was Fischer's Blue Room and Bar and then a restaurant, a used car lot and garage and a cream station. Wagner's Butcher Shop and Groceries, a bank building and an implement store were next. The final businesses were a lumberyard, grain elevators and the stock yards.

Strasburg was a popular center for anniversary celebrations, weddings and dances of all kinds. On Easter Monday the biggest dance of the year was held. Usually John Schwab played for it in the Blue Room. There were no dances during Lent, a time for prayer and fasting. The pavilion at Seeman Park in Linton also served as a popular dance hall throughout the year.

For people in "My First World" fuel for burning was a dominant commodity. Lignite coal was mined in North Dakota but the cost was from $1.50 to $3.00 a ton. In the 1930's, anything over 50¢ was considered to be high priced. To supplement coal, the farmers turned to other sources. Cow chips were harvested from pastures and stored for winter. Corn cobs produced a swift flame. During the summer months, kerosene burning stoves were used. There was another way to make fuel--from barn manure. All of the winter barn cleanings were put into a pile away from the barn. Around May, this pile was spread out to a twelve-inch thickness. Horses were lead over this spread for hours until it was trampled down and hard. The spread, then perhaps five inches thick, was left for a week or more in the sun and wind to dry. After the correct drying had occurred the manure was cut with a spade into eight inch squares, much like you would cut a cake in a pan. After one more week of drying, the squares were lifted out and piled into small stacks to dry even more. Finally, the squares were stacked onto a pile and, bingo, there was artificial coal.

Most farmers in "My First World" had outdoor cellars. They harvested ice in the winter from Beaver Creek and dams and stored it in the cellars for summer. Ice cream was a super treat. However cellars without ice were also quite cool for cream and butter storage in the summer. Smoke cured pork often hung in these cellars. These cellars offered shelter during wind and thunderstorms and the gruesome summer heat of the 1930s. My father built a smoke house and fuel storage building that had walls made from flat field rock and clay mortar. The mortar was fun to make. I trampled with bare feet and legs in the clay, water and straw mixture until it became a homogenous smear. The finished structure received a coat of white-wash.

Another shelter which these creative Germans built was a straw barn, warm in the winter and cool in the summer. This was comfortable for any farm animal. The walls were made of pig wire fence, two feet apart and stuffed tightly with straw. The roof of this straw shelter consisted of rows of pig wire and straw weighted down with old tires and supported by wooden poles.　　＊＊＊＊＊

BOSCH'S AND SEEMAN

Andrew Bosch lived the farthest west of all the Rosenthal parishioners. Elizabeth was his wife and they had nine children, John, Ignatz, Alex, Philipena, Elizabeth, Margaret, Frances, Theresa and Andrew. Ignatz died in 1935. He had a son, Henry, who attended the Precious Blood Seminary in Canton, Ohio. Henry left there and became a priest for the Diocese of Bismarck. Father Henry Bosch died while serving the church in Mott.

The fifth Bosch brother was Ignatz. Apparently there was not enough land on Beaver Creek for all five Bosch brothers. Ignatz lived on Highway 13 just below a large hill and was known as "Ignatz on the Hill." His wife Margaret, bore Ignatz, Jr., Valentine, Leopold, Andrew, Marcus, Tony, Kathy, Eugenia, Nickodemus and Caroline.

Two of these children were lost to diphtheria, an awful, infectious disease, before the discovery of penicillin. Families who had this disease were quarantined for a long period of time. A statement which I remember old Ignatz making one Sunday pertained to his opinion on the CCC program. He said he would never let his boys join the CCC because they dressed in military clothes. He had a right to think that way. Many other people thought that way too because not to many years before the Russian government reneged on military service exemptions. For generations the people of "My First World" took the back seat with government authorities and learned to mistrust them.

Joe Hager and his wife, Katie, lived on the Petrie farm west of Andrew Bosch on Beaver Creek. Their children were Mike, Joe, Jean, Betty, Anton and Ann. This farm stretched toward Seeman Park in Linton. Seeman Park was named after the man who donated the land for it, L.D. Seeman. He came to Emmons County in 1906 and became its largest land owner. He bought and shipped several thousand head of cattle and horses annually. He was a nice man and treated farmers well. One time my father sold him a horse before spring's work. Mr. Seeman allowed the horse to be used for plowing and seeding before he came to get it. Sometimes my father elected to drive sold cattle to Linton instead of paying to truck them. I loved the pony riding, the neighbor boys would ride their ponies too and help herd the cattle to town. It was a slow process, taking hours. Hurrying the cattle along would have caused them to lose too many pounds before wieghing at the stock yards in Linton. Mr. Seeman dealt in grain elevators, farming, garage and auto sales and was a founder of the Linton Livestock Sales. He was one of the first directors of the First National Bank in Linton. He also donated land to the Linton Public School.   * * * * *

FARMS - LINTON

The farm west of mine belonged to Adam and Magdalina Wolf. Their eleven children were Magdalina, Anton, Ignatius, John, Phyllis, Mike, Christine, Peter, Barbara, Joseph and Albert. They were friendly neighbors and we visited each others homes. Their land touched my farm and Joe and Albert were gopher catching buddies of mine. They had a nice big pony named "Butte." Most of the Wolf children went to high school and many of them went to college. Their school was to the west of their farm, but Adam sent many of his children to the Catholic school in Strasburg because of his unusual interest in a good education. Adam was also into politics and government. He once said that when he was younger he thought you could never get into heaven unless you were a Democrat and a Catholic. But as he got older he found that this was not true. You didn't have to be a Catholic. He also said that in all of his Bible readings he never read that Jesus rode into town on an elephant. Adam's farming prowess was not what attracted me to him, it was his administrative and educational talents. As I said previously in this writing, Adam was not a farmer by choice but rather by necessity. The Catholic schools in Strasburg had top-notch teachers in the nuns and priests who emphasized the importance of high school and college. They were often successful in guiding students to higher scholastic goals, especially if the student had cooperative parents. Albert was a classmate of mine at St. Thomas College in St. Paul and today is a prominent lawyer in Bismarck.

South of Adam Wolfs, near the road to Strasburg lived Wendelin and Barbara Wickenheiser. Their children were Bertha, Eleanor, Aloys, Raymond, William, Victoria and Clarence. Aloys was a playmate of mine and we visited fairly often. Wendelin was a brother of Mrs. Adam Wolf.

The next farm in "My First World" was that of Jack and Elizabeth Bauman. Their offspring were Pete, Margaret, Tony, Benny, Loretta and Iggie. Benny and Iggie were friends of mine. Tony was killed in World War II in Europe. Jack Bauman was the son of Sebastian Bauman, one of the original scouts from Russia in 1888. Bauman's were very nice to me. Later, during my college summers, I worked for their threshing crew. That was fun because of the camaraderie and the enormous amounts of good food they served. Baumans threshed my father's farm after 1941.

The final farm south, before Strasburg, belonged to Carl and Catherine Keller, no relation to me. They had more children than anyone in "My First World"---eighteen and one died. Their names were Mary, Agatha, Barbara, Eugene, Aloys, Helen, Cecilia, Hilda, Genieva, Ursala, Charlie, Bernedette, Bobby, Henrietta, Harlene, Katie and Anton. They had a huge, square, two-storied white house. Their barn was also white and beautiful with Holstein cows around it. I looked forward to seeing that farm when we went to Strasburg.

I spent the 1940-1941 school year attending Linton High School, my sister, Mary, and I first boarded with a Mrs. Rohrich and later joined Joe, Rose and Maggie Klein in the basement apartment of people named Schulz. Our apartment had a kitchen-living room combined, two bedrooms and a bath. The adjustment from farm school to town

120

high school was enormous. In town the grade school terms were nine months compared to seven months on the farm. My English language skills were poor. Two classmates from town school whom I liked very much were Clement Herred and Tyler Hubbard. Clement's father ran the light plant in Linton. He also had a job on the local Draft Board for World War II in 1941. Years later, I met Clement while he was attending the University of Minnesota Dental School and I was attending St. Thomas College in St. Paul. Tyler became a high ranking Naval officer in World War II.

My Social Studies teacher was Mrs. Lilja. She was very encouraging to me. She could find reasons to compliment me in many ways. Her husband was a barber in Linton. Miss Goldade was my English teacher, not an easy job for her. Mr. Bob Carlson was a coach and an administrator. I never felt complete or comfortable that year. I didn't feel as though I was learning much. The following September Father Charles Meyer opened the education gates for me by taking me to Canton, Ohio in his 1941 Ford where I started high school all over again. I moved nine hundred miles and as many cultures away from "My First World".

* * * * *

FROM ALSACE TO STRASBURG

Allow me now to give a partial summary and a few thoughts on the origination of my forefathers. The very beginning was in Alsace-Lorraine, a region in northeastern France on the French-German border. Mostly Roman-Catholic, Alsace-Lorraine has been part German and part French for hundreds of years. Conquerors have crossed Alsace-Lorraine many times. In the years during the 300 and 400's. Teutonic (Germanic) bands drove out the Celtic tribes then living there. In the 700's it became part of Charlemagne's Empire. It fell to Germany when his grandsons divided the empire. Alsace-Lorraine remained German until the 1500's when France again gained control. In 1871 the Germans retrieved it again. The Germans resented the loss of Alsace-Lorraine after World War I and regained possession in World War II. The Allies drove the Germans out of Alsace-Lorraine in 1944-1945 and today the territory belongs to France.

When my ancestors left Alsace-Lorraine in about 1802, Germany had been overrun by Napoleon and the Prussian rulers were trying to unify Germany. They were exploiting people and conscripting them for military service. Political strife and general unrest stirred my ancestor's ears towards the east when Catherine of Russia called for Germans to come to her country. As stated in this writing, she offered them "Crown Land" and exemption from military conscription.

My ancestors left Germany from the city of Ulm and floated down the Danube River to Vienna, Austria. From there they traveled overland to Odessa, Russia on the Black Sea. All in all it was a 1,680 mile trip and took about four months. Of the three migrating groups of Germans; Catholics, Mennonites and Lutheran Evangelicals, the Catholics were assigned to the Kutschurgan on the Kutschurgan River on the Black Sea. They formed six settlements, Kandel, Selz, Baden, Strasburg, Manheim and Elsas. Although most of these Germans were doctors, teachers, merchants, tradesmen and artists, they were very successful farmers in Russia. They soon rented more land and then bought this rented land. Russian natives began to complain about the Germans taking over. The Russian Czar Alexander was made aware of these aggressive Germans and in 1871 he decreed to "Russiafy" his country. He began to conscript Germans for the Russian-Japanese War, denied them land ownership and freedom of religious worship. As they became peasants their lifestyle disintegrated. There was no longer education for their children. To add to the political pollution, Lenin was inventing Communism in Russia and threatening the Czar.

Again, my ancestors were ripe for a new homeland. The opportunity to emigrate from Russia arose when the United States offered them land in Dakota Territory. Coming to America my ancestors traveled overland by railroad to Hamburg, Germany and then by ship to New York. They processed through Ellis Island. Two years ago, Shirley and I visited Ellis Island. A museum there contains piles of wooden and metal trunks, lost baggage that went unclaimed 100 years ago by these immigrants. (So modern airlines didn't invent lost baggage after all!) From New York my ancestors traveled to Eureka, South Dakota by train and by oxcart to Strasburg, North Dakota. At this time, about 1880, the United States was only about 100 years old. It was the only country in the world founded on the principles of individual human rights. In its founding principles, it was the most moral country on earth. These freedoms enabled my ancestors, in their tremendous struggles, to build churches and schools and to provide for themselves and their large families. They knew that these freedoms would enable their descendants to again become teachers, doctors, merchants, governors, presidents, lawyers, priests, or to remain farmers, but the choice was theirs. They knew that the

United States of America was a far better country than any of their ancestors ever could have imagined in the 300's, 1500's, 1700's, or 1800's.

In knowing the history of my ancestors, I can understand myself better in the present and am more able to ponder the future.

I enjoyed writing this. As Anne Frank said in her book, *The Diary of Anne Frank*, "paper is patient."   * * * * *

HARD TIMES

In "My First World" the farms consisted of about 400 acres of land. They were stocked with twelve to fifteen milk cows, and, in all, about thirty head of cattle. There were five to ten hogs, seventy to ninety chickens, some turkeys and ducks. Each farm had twelve to twenty horses. All these animals provided food, power and transportation to work the land and feed the people. Children made up a large part of the work force. Four to five people could do the milking in half an hour, then separate and store the cream in the outdoor cellar for Saturday's trip to town. Harnessing and hitching horse teams was performed easily by eleven and twelve year old children. Families spent all day together. The land was lived on, memorized, learned and enjoyed. People were married to the land, cared for it tenderly and loved it.

Late 1929 and the very early 1930's brought with them the economic effects of the Great Depression. Good crops brought very low prices; wheat at 25¢ a bushel. In 1934, the rains almost completely stopped for four years. Spring after spring farmers planted wheat and corn only to see the fields blackened and destroyed by dust storms and grasshoppers. Dirt clouds blackened the sky during daylight hours. Mounds of dust gathered on the thistle stuffed fences making it possible for me to walk right over a fence. Blowing dust struck against buildings and formed banks on the ground. During blizzard days there was a constant dust between one's teeth, in one's nose and ears. Farmers wore handkerchiefs over their nose and mouth, and goggles over their eyes while working in the fields. Dust settled in all areas of our house. The water pail that contained the dipper for drinking had a large layer of dust on its bottom. Mending fences required the application of water to the ground so fence posts could be placed. There were inch-wide cracks where the earth had split open. Grasshoppers traveled in clouds so thick that they blocked out the sun and formed mounds around buildings as they hit the walls and fell to the ground. Government programs paid for the spread of grasshoppers poison along fences and pastures. Hogs and chickens then fed on the dead, poisoned hoppers and they, too, died. Farm animals starved to death. Thistles and wild onions thrived in the dry soil and were harvested as hay. This poor substitute constipated horses causing their death. I often chased our horses with my pony for hours hoping to move their bowels so they could live. Starving cattle were driven to Strasburg where the government paid $5.00 a head and then destroyed them in the city dump. Franklin D. Roosevelt was our president then and government help was prevalent. Government programs such as NYA (National Youth Association), CCC (Civilian Conservation Corps), and WPA (Works Progress Administration) gave jobs to people of all ages. WPA employed men for road and public parks construction. The CCC employed men sixteen years old and older in semi-military camps to build dams, and national and local buildings. A CCC dam was built on Frank Hagel's property. NYA employed women who sewed shirts and trousers to give away. Food commodities were regularly distributed in Linton. A Mrs. Leuwer was in charge of that program. Apples, oranges, grapefruit, pears, prunes, peas, dried beans, and canned meat were among the different kinds of foods distributed. Add to that sugar and flour, and the people in "My First World" could live forever.

* * * * *

THRESHING AND BUTCHERING

Peter Kraft and his wife, Julia, also had a good crop of offspring---thirteen. They lived in the vicinity too. Their children were Margaret, Mike, Mary, Andy, Joe, Alice, Maggie, Eddie, Helen, Lorraine, Leonard, Jake and Sister Margaret Alice. Eddie and Leonard were my playmates. Their parents often visited our home. The Krafts owned a threshing machine and threshed grain for other farmers. During the harvests of 1932, 1933, 1938, 1939, 1940 and 1941 they threshed the grain on our farm. During harvest, grain stocks were cut by a header and stacked onto piles of twos, fours or sixes, side by side. They were left to dry for two or three weeks. Then the threshing machine would move between two stacks and the stocks of wheat were pitched into the machine by four men. The grain came out on one side of the machine and the straw blew out the back of the machine to make huge piles. The grain was transported in wagons to granaries on the farm or to elevators in Strasburg or Linton. This was a most exciting time for me; harnessing and driving teams of horses and bringing lunches (store-bought bread with Kraft cheese sandwiches) to the field. There were two lunches daily in the field and three meals at the house. Everybody was busy from 4:30 a.m. until 10:30 p.m. For about three to four days there were approximately ten men at our farm working. Women worked harder than the men; preparing food, doing farm chores and taking care of the children. It was a happy time for me as well as the pay-off time for the year. A good wheat crop ran twenty bushels an acre, barley ran thirty and oats forty bushels an acre. No one ever fertilized the ground with chemicals then and horse-drawn plows only dug five-inch furrows. The end of threshing time meant the end of big summer farm work and for me the beginning of another school term, a happy time of the year for me.

Another cooperative get-together for farmers was butchering in the fall. The people in "My First World" were enormous pork eaters. Beef was used only to make borscht soup or to mix in with pork to make meat patties. Chicken, too, was very popular but was always butchered on the day it was used. On butchering day, neighbors came with their favorite knives. Wendelin Klein also brought his pistol to make the first part easy. Four or five pigs would be butchered. After the kill they would be dumped into a tub of boiling water, then hung from the barn rafters by their hind legs, hair cleaned off and gutted. The carcasses were divided into their desired sections and carried into the house for further processing. The intestines and stomach were cleaned and used for sausage and headcheese. There were three kinds of sausage; liver was added to make liver sausage, blood was added to make blood sausage and then their was just plain sausage, rings and rings and rings of it. Headcheese contained bits of skin, the ears, tongue and miscellaneous scraps packed into the stomach, compressed and boiled. This was a delicacy eaten cold. I liked to dip headcheese into vinegar. All of the sausage, hams and headcheese were smoked, cured and hung in the cellar. When beef was butchered, two or three farmers would split one because beef was harder to keep during

127

the winter. It had to be wrapped and buried under wheat in the granary. Most times we just bought fresh beef over the counter. I never saw an entire butchering operation because it was always on a school day but I could hardly wait to come home to see the excitement. The camaraderie among adults as they worked was priceless to my good feelings.

* * * * *

SEMINARY HIGH SCHOOL

Father Meyer often visited and dined with the parishioners. In 1941 he ended my stay in "My First World" by taking me to Canton, Ohio. He gave me a free ticket to the world of education. When Father Charles entered the United States Army the following year he sent his typewriter to me to use. That was an unforgettable gesture of support for me.

The three Precious Blood Community priests I knew at Rosenthal were dedicated, religious, hardworking men. The Precious Blood Community believed in high scholastics, physical labor and good social habits while training their priests. The minor seminary in Ohio was on a four hundred acre farm managed and worked by priests, students and brothers. The students stayed there for twelve months out of the year. All of the meat, milk and produce needed was produced on the farm. Acres of potatoes, pumpkins, melons, apples, peaches, pears, cherries, grapes and all vegetables were harvested and stored for use.

If I can take a few sentences here to tell you what this seminary is today you would all recognize the signs of the times. This once-prospering seminary building with its four hundred acres is now the Glenmoore Country Club. A developer in Canton,

Ohio bought it and had Jack Nicklaus build an 18-hole golf course. The fairways are ringed with beautiful homes. The seminary building constructed in 1931 was entirely preserved. Classrooms, study halls, dormitory rooms and the library are now condominiums. The priest's rooms are overnight guest rooms. The refectory became the ladies' locker room and shower, and the washrooms and gym became the mens' locker room. The chapel area is now a huge formal dining room and the twelve individual side altars are private dining areas. The main altar was replaced with a giant fireplace and the Sacristy by the kitchen area. Last of all, the choir loft is now a lounge overlooking the dining space. A spring-fed lake in front of the building which was once used for swimming, skating, boating and fishing is now the signature golf hole with a water carry from tee to green. In the back of the building is the drive-out sub-basement which was once a storage area for produce. It now houses the fleet of motorized golf carts. The basement with back entrance contains the Pro Shop and golf bag storage.

If you have $25,000 and are willing to wait in line for years, you may become a member of the Glenmoore Country Club.

* * * * *

EARLY GRADE SCHOOL

Wells School was located on Beaver Creek. I always wished I could have lived on Beaver Creek. We played there often during school free time. It was such a big fun playground. The water, trees and bushes were settled with rabbits, snakes, pheasants, prairie chickens, turtles, fish and crabs under the rocks in the shallow water. The bushes and trees bore berries, cherries, plums and chestnuts. There were flowers and cactus and thorny bushes. Different earth formations were exciting "Hide-and-Seek" sites. We skated on the ice. We harvested little Y-shaped branches for sling shots and larger branches to make stilts.

My first grade teacher in 1932 was Miss Wells. She was a nice lady, slender with dark hair and a spit curl on her forehead. On the first day of school she wore a red dress. Miss Wells was different from any lady I had ever known. She was not a farm wife with children. She was from some city I thought. I loved to watch her eat lunch. Her lunch pail was not like our syrup pails and her sandwiches were not syrup bread. Her lunch pail was black with silver snaps and a silver handle on top. It contained a thermos with coffee and her sandwiches were store-bought sliced bread with green leaf lettuce. I wasn't sure if lettuce was for sandwiches but she looked so nice eating it.

Miss Wells was very patient and kind to me and my classmates. Eugenia Vetter, Joe Vetter and Joe Klein. None of us could speak English. She would point to the blackboard and we would say "blackboard." Then she would say "desk" and we would say "desk" and so on. She would skip and we would say "skip". A teacher's job was monumental and it was all accomplished to varying degrees. School held such enjoyment for me. Christmas plays with my parents present and school picnics were most exciting events.

Until I reached the fifth grade, each student had only one book, a "Reader." The teacher had a "Speller", a poem book and an arithmetic book from which she wrote all of the work onto the blackboard for us to copy. This all changed in the fifth grade when one day a truck brought more books than I had ever seen---ever. The books were all colors, sizes and of many subjects: Geography, Agriculture, Math, Social Studies, Reading and Poem books. They smelled good and their bindings cracked as I opened them. I had never felt a new book until that day. Our "Readers" had all been hand-me-downs. Something changed inside me that day. I strongly sensed someone cared very much for us children. I was more exhilarated than ever about school. My text book surprise came when I started my first year of high school in Linton in September, 1940, and saw entire walls covered with books in the school library. The poem books I mentioned above played a big part in my grade school education. I constantly memorized poems and to this exercise I contribute much of my success in school in later life. It was a good memory training.   * * * * *

CHURCH ACTIVITIES

All of the people in "My Seven Square Miles" were Catholic, most belonged to Rosenthal Parish, Church of the Sacred Heart. The people closer to Strasburg belonged to Saints Peter and Paul in Strasburg. There were families who attended Rosenthal parish and lived east of "My Seven Square Miles." I did not know those farms but some of the names were Kramer, Stoppler, Jangula, Horner, Kuhn, Ell, Vetter, Bosch, Grensteiner, Ibach and Schneider. Socially, spiritually and psychologically the church was an enormous part of everyone in "My First World". Church was where people were baptized, received First Holy Communion, were confirmed, married and buried. On church days people came early and stayed late, visited and socialized. Women gathered in the church foyer and in cars. Men were grouped along the side of the church and the children were in cars and on the church grounds. During the winter the men gathered below the church around the coal furnace to visit. Everyone attended all church functions whether it was a wedding, a regular Sunday, a funeral or just a Rosary or Catechism service. Church fairs were held on the John Horner farm. John had a granary the size of a civic center, or so it seemed to me then. There were raffle wheels, Bingo, ring throws and other games. Corn kernels were used for Bingo card markers. Much food was served and a fun time was held by all. Politicians visited these celebrations. The most famous politician was Bill Langer, Governor of North Dakota and a United States Congressman. By the way, Langer cast the sole vote against World War II in 1941. During these local visits Langer dressed like "one of us". He demonstrated poverty to the extent of a broken shoe lace dragging on the floor. Many parishioners were "Langer Men" and welcomed him.

"Hungry, Bill?" was a question I remember hearing the farmers ask him while he was eating. These happy social occasions produced a few dollars for the church, but they were mostly a lot of fun for children and adults.

* * * * *

MASS

I served Mass starting at age seven until I left at age fourteen (1927-1941). I loved to serve weddings the most. There was a fun custom at weddings which had the servers taking up a collection for themselves at the door as the wedding party was leaving the church. People threw coins into our caps.

Funerals were the least fun to serve. For me they were emotionally devastating. Caskets were brought to the church in a Model T truck owned by a Bosch who lived east of the church. After the church services, six men carried the casket to the cemetery and all the people followed behind. Our German pioneers were prone to wailing and talking to the deceased. At the cemetery the casket was lowered and young men shoveled dirt into the grave. Everyone stayed, what seemed to me forever, until the grave was filled with earth.

The funeral service always had an ample supply of incense burning and it was my job to hold the incense boat on a chain. This heavy scent would stay with me for days after and continuously remind me of those not-so-happy occasions. I thought all funerals were this way until the first one I encountered after I left "My First World." It was the funeral of an old priest in the Precious Blood Seminary in Ohio. I was absolutely astounded to see not even one tear and plenty of smiles at the funeral.

The Feast of the Sacred Heart was always a big celebration at Rosenthal parish. The date was June 14th. On that special day families from neighboring parishes in Linton, Strasburg, St. Aloysious, Hague and Krassna (west of Strasburg) attended our church. The priests and their housemaids also attended. The visiting priests concelebrated the Mass. I enjoyed the priests talking to us servers before Mass. The church was crowded and the choir sang beautifully, the same Mass they always sang, but louder. The Mass was "*Missa de Angelis*", (*Mass of the Angels*) the only one they knew.

One change in the music for that special day was the final hymn; "*O Groser Gott Wier Loben Dich*", (*Holy God We Praise Thy Name*). This song was saved for special occasions and was the only time congregational singing was encouraged and it was always extremely loud.

After Mass the priests and their maids went to the parish priest's house for dinner. Visiting families joined parishioners in their homes for dinner. My mother always took pride in this dinner; chicken soup, mashed potatoes, gravy, beef and lemon meringue pie with graham cracker crust.

"*Missa de Angelis*" was the only Mass I ever heard in "My First World."

I thought this was **THE** Catholic Mass. I remember writing home from Ohio that the Mass we were singing there didn't sound Catholic. To pursue this thought a year later our music teacher, Father Fred Cook, said he was introducing a new Mass for us to learn, "*Missa de Angelis*". He later marveled how fast I learned this piece of music, "Keller, you certainly caught on to this one," he remarked.

At Rosenthal different musical people served as organists. Ignatius Kuhn, Ignatz Bosch and Tony Hagel played the organ and led the choir during my years there. These men also led the Rosary before Mass and taught Catechism during summer school at Wells #18 for a three week summer session.

* * * * *

QUEENS OF THE PRAIRIE

Of course the farm homes in "My First World" did not have indoor plumbing. This had a serious impact on hygiene, laundry and cooking. All water was carried from the well to the house and heated on the stove. There were no weekly baths, only weekly head and feet washing. Baths were reserved for Christmas and Easter. During the summer months the creeks and dams served as bathing facilities. Teeth were seldom, if ever, treated to a brush. A toothache called for an automatic extraction either by parents

134

or Dr. Edwin Mork. All clothing changes were weekly at best. With as large of families as everyone had then, laundry days were a huge undertaking. Some people had Maytag engine machines. Enormous tubs of hot water were transferred to the washing machine from the stove. Some laundry was done on washboards. Then came the drying. Clothes lines were filled again and again. During the winter the laundry froze on the lines, so it was hung up all over the inside of the house. Monday was wash day at home and I do not have fond memories of that chore.

Baking bread consumed another day for the mother's of the house. My father often took sacks of wheat to a flour mill in Temvik, a little town just north of Linton. It was there that the wheat was turned into flour. For baking day the dough was started the night before in large basins. In this one day these wonderful mothers would turn out a weeks supply of ten to twenty large loaves in the bellies of coal, manure or weed-fed stoves. It was like a miracle. Bread was the dominant food served at each meal. My forefathers held two things in their hands while they ate: one hand held a fork, the other a piece of bread.

Sometimes a side dish on baking day was "Dumpf Noodles". Little balls of bread dough were placed in a roaster with lard and some water on the bottom and were steamed. The bottom layer became very crispy and the dish was served with stewed prunes. Another dish similar to this one was finger-sized noodles from a different kind of dough. It was prepared in a roaster too but with added potatoes or sauerkraut. Food prepared from flour was very prominent, cheese buttons and dumplings of all sorts. Potatoes were a twice a day ritual. Blachinda was a great pastry dish made with pumpkin filling and a thinly spread flour dough. Blachinda and bean soup were the greatest of combinations.

Without indoor plumbing and electricity the women in "My First World" labored through incredibly long hard days. Laundering, ironing and mending mounds of clothes, baking, cooking, gardening, cleaning house, much of the milking chores and some of the field work were all a part of a woman's duties. One has to remember that these women were pregnant most of the time and they had other children to look after too. What seems like insurmountable tasks were routine for these "Queens of the Prairie." These heroines drew strength from the examples of their mothers and from their religion. The Church taught them that this was the will of God and their duty. They were mostly humble and unusually focused on their work.

In "My First World" women did not drive cars. This seriously inhibited their mobility. A few women joined the convent where they were hugely revered by the Church. In the convent their life was much easier and they enjoyed the constant praise and honor of their parents and relatives. The Catholic church had an overwhelming influence over the people of "My First World." If there was a "down" side to this almost unnatural authority, women harbored the greater share. Men often drowned their frustrations with alcohol and tobacco use while women were not allowed such indulgences. I am sure the psychological health of women was tested many times.

* * * * *

BEAVER CREEK FARMERS

Back in "My First World" the farm just west of the Red Bridge was that of George Bosch. George was one of five brothers who settled along Beaver Creek. The Bosch's spoke with a different German dialect and were nicknamed "Crimers" because they were from the Crimean area of Russia. The rest of the people in "My First World" were nicknamed "Odessers" because they were from Odessa, Russia. George and his wife, Philipena, had seven children; Margaret, Elizabeth, Peter, Catherine, Rose, Mary and Theresa. Peter was married and had three children with whom I went to school,. Margaret, Rose and Frances. They used to ride from school with me in my one horse, two-wheeled trailer as far as Hagel's corner. During the summer, I often walked to the creek on George's land to pick chokecherries. In his pasture there was always a spirited bull who demanded respect as he protected his herd.

As we follow the creek westward, Anton and Catherina Kelsch had a farm. Their many children were Katie, Linda, Mary, Frances, Jake, Pius, Rosalie, Betty, Tony and Caroline. Tony was a playmate to my older brothers and went to school with me. He then went to Linton High School and played football for the school team. I often listened as he described his school experiences, what he was learning in high school impressed me. On one particular occasion, he told of the United States importing sugar, spice and indigo. As he said "indigo" he spurred his horse and off he went. Rosalie was a housemaid to Father Charles Meyer. In 1942, when Father Charles left for World War II, she entered the convent. The Kelsches had a very nice blue 1929 Chrysler with pull-down canvas curtains on the windows and wooden spokes on the wheels.

The next farm on the creek was that of John Schiele. His wife was named Catherine and their five children were Edward, Herman, Kathy, Tony and Bernie. During winter months we passed their farm as we traveled cross country to Linton with horses and sled. The Schiele children and everyone west of them attended the school on Highway 13. But I came to know them through church and summer Catechism school.

Anton and Christine Bosch had eight children and lived next on the creek. The offspring here were John, Katherine, Magdalina, Joe, Elizabeth, Caroline, Jake and Tony. Magdelina was my mother's age. They befriended one another when my mother came to Rosenthal after she married my father in 1917. Magdelina later married a Wald and moved to Napoleon. Her son, Frank Wald, today is a prominent State Legislator from Dickinson. Tony came to our house sometimes to visit my brothers and sisters.

The next farm west was that of Fred and Magdelina Bosch. They raised seven children; Steve, Clemence, Fred, Pius, Katherine, Johanna and Philipena. Fred, Jr. was an organist at Rosenthal.

* * * * *

TEACHERS - GODMOTHER - MISSED TALENTS

All of the teachers boarded with neighboring farm families. Miss Wells stayed at the Wendalin Klein farm. Rosina and Mary Eva Vetter were two more of my teachers and boarded with their brother, Frank Vetter's family. Frank lived just south of the school. He and his wife, Jenny, had eight children; Joe, Eugenia, Leo, Virginia, Frank, Mary, Tony and Tim. Rosina was a very strict, stern teacher. Her sister, Mary Eva, was patient and mellow. She "got off the subject" many times during class and told of interesting events she had read and heard about. A story she told one day was especially exciting to me. A nephew of hers, Frank Horner, had gone to Linton High School after farm school. Few students ever went on to high school then. Her nephew even went to the University of Minnesota and became an engineer. Right then I knew that I too was going to go to school somewhere else someday.

Mrs. McGee was another teacher of mine. She was a sturdy lady, tender and fair, who boarded also at Wendalin Klein's home. Wendalin and his wife, Bridget, were very warm people to me. Bridget was my Godmother and always paid much attention to me. A quarter wrapped in tinfoil on the bottom of a Christmas candy bag made a lasting impression on me. I passed through the Klein's farmyard every day on the way to school. Her treats included "a slice around the loaf" jelly bread. Klein's children were Andy, Lizzy, Magdalina, Rose and Joe. Joe usually rode down the hill to school with me in our sled, wagon or trailer. Andy had gone to high school in Strasburg and then on to business college and a good job in an Aberdeen, South Dakota lumber yard. I was most impressed. Wendalin stood out among the farmers in "My First World" because he was "bookish". He was known to read a book while driving a team of horses during field work. There was usually only one opportunity to make a living for most of these early pioneers in "My First World", that was farming. People could have excelled in education had they only had the opportunity to do so.

Mr. Klein, Adam Wolf and my mother come to mind when I speak of missed talents. My mother loved to read and was very interested in the outside world. She often bought a paper, "*The Grit*", which had world news and pictures. I remember three of these stories. One was about Bruno Richard Kauptman. He had been convicted of kidnapping and killing the Lindberg child. Pictures showed him being paraded through the streets of Chicago with people watching from the rooftops. Another showed the gangster John Dillinger being shot by police while leaving a theater in Chicago. The third picture was so gruesome that my stomach still feels tight when I think of it. It was of a firing squad executing a man, blindfolded and tied to a post, in Mexico. All of these stories were in woeful contrast to the lifestyle which I knew in "My First World", but they told me something about the rest of the world. Getting back to Mr. Klein, he often stood on an overlook to the creek and watched us school children skate on the ice. He was a portly, mustached man with a constant pipe in his mouth and an open jacket.

* * * * *

ROOTS

A favorite author of mine, James Michener, once said, "Your roots are where your mother and father lived and died." My roots may be in Emmons County, North Dakota, but "My First World" is a "Seven Square Mile" area (see map enclosed) bounded by Highway 83 and the Milwaukee Railroad tracks from Strasburg to Linton, Highway 13 from Linton east to Horner's corner, the graveled section line road south over the Red Bridge on Beaver Creek, past Hagel's corner, Well's School #18 and Rosenthal Parish Church, further south past Keller's mailbox on to Schwab's corner and southwest to Strasburg. My parents were Frank and Helen Keller. My mother's father was Debertius Schneider. They lived in Hague, North Dakota and he was a blacksmith. My grandfather and my uncle, Louis Schneider forged most of the iron crosses found in cemeteries in Hague, Strasburg, Linton and Rosenthal. The book *"Iron Spirits"*, by the

North Dakota Council on Arts, contains an early family picture of my grandparents on page 50. The oldest girl in the picture is my mother. My uncle, Louis Schneider is pictured on page 57.

Wilma, Mary and Eleanor were my sisters and Frank, Debert and Willie were my brothers. My home was somewhat in the midst of this "Seven Square Mile" tract. I experienced the first fourteen years of my life here, from 1927 until 1941. I knew all the farm homes and the people who inhabited these parameters. I met them all many times in my association with school, church, Linton and Strasburg. Inhibited mobility kept me inside these boundaries except for occasional visits to grandparents in Bismarck and Fort Yates.

One of these trips to Bismarck was memorable. My father and I had left Bismarck to return home. About three miles out of town we noticed a huge fire in Bismarck. We stopped the car and got out to observe it. I can remember the tall weeds along the road being between my eyes and the fire. I was a very little boy then. It was 1930, the North Dakota State Capital building was burning.

A trip to Fort Yates meant crossing the Missouri River on a rickety old ferry boat. Captain Thompson fired up his steam engine at the sound of a horn on the opposite side, then came chugging after the waiting passengers. He was a skinny old leathery man who lived on his steamboat, drank river water, and fried fish in his kitchen. To me, he was total amusement.

I love the "My First World" area and often visit it. I love to walk on the land and drive through it. I can feel the spirits of my forefathers whose bones rest there. I especially love my farm home land. I remember every hill and valley, the large unmovable rocks, the gopher and badger hole areas, the cactus patches, pot holes, chokecherry and juneberry groves, and the rock piles I played on at my farm. My forefathers would be completely astounded to know that large field rocks, once a total hindrance to farm land, are being sold today by lawn decorating businesses for $50.00 to $150.00 a piece. As a child I was often alone with my land, but never lonesome. I always had my friends; my pony, the gophers, rabbits, cows, calves, birds, chickens, ducks, pigs, goats, cats, and dogs to be with, to listen for and to. There were the sounds of the prairies; tractors, machinery, trains, wind, thunder, airplanes, church bells, or just the quiet stillness. * * * * *

CHURCHES

The ten acres of ground that was the church yard and cemetery was donated by John Vetter, the father of Frank and Mike Vetter. The first church building, built in 1907, was destroyed a year later, in 1908, by a wind storm. By snow fall the farmers had rebuilt the new church. My grandfather, Mike Keller, drove to Aberdeen, South Dakota in his one horse buggy to collect money from fellow Germans from Russia in that area to rebuild the church. Grandpa Keller donated three of his heifer cows.

As you entered the center isle of the church, the women sat on the left and the men sat on the right. Children sat in front and adults to the rear. Beyond the communion rail was the altar with the priest and alter boys. The choir loft was upstairs in the back, with a "state of the art" pump organ for the choir. Everybody wore Sunday clothes to church. Boys and men wore suits, white shirts, ties, and dress shoes. Girls and women were in dresses, hats and nice shoes. There was always a definite sense of order, respect, pride and reverence.

Around the time that the Rosenthal parish was formed, there was some friction in a parish three miles northeast of the future town of Strasburg. The parish church was Saints Peter and Paul in a community called Tiraspol. In the spring of 1902, the Chicago, Milwaukee and St. Paul railroad came through Emmons County, three miles west of Saints Peter and Paul Church. Businesses built around the railroad and the town of Strasburg was born. The church was out in the country and there was discord among the parishioners as to whether to move the church or leave it in the country. The church was moved into Strasburg and many of the people to the north of the church joined Rosenthal parish. As the parish house was moved, it broke in half smack on the railroad tracks, with half on one side and half on the town side. Just then a train came along, stopped, cleared away the debris on the tracks and moved right through the house which was later reassembled at the new location in Strasburg. The Tiraspol Cemetery is near the Carl Keller farm. A list of our ancestry buried there is included here. I obtained this list of interred from the "*Johannes Baumgartner Story and Genealogy*", Bicentennial Edition 1774 - 1974 written by John Baumgartner III.

* * * * *

FOREFATHERS

In the fall of 1888, my forefathers decided to send a scouting team of five men from the Russian colony of Strasburg to Dakota Territory in America. The five men who arrived in Eureka, South Dakota and went on to Emmons County were Joseph

Baumgartner, Joseph Burgad, Sebastian Bauman, Jacob Feist and Joseph Kraft. The young men kept their relatives and friends in Russia informed of the conditions on these new plains and urged them to come to Dakota Territory.

On May 7th, 1889, eleven families from Russia arrived in Dakota Territory. This group was disheartened by a huge prairie fire that had blackened thousands of acres just prior to their arrival. The country looked completely black, prairie rocks were glittering in the sun like diamonds on a black gown. On the evening of their arrival they were greeted by a frightening thunder and lightening storm. They threw their wagon boxes upside down onto the ground and took shelter under them.

Persistent, and not to be denied, my forefathers adapted, as was their nature, and built sod shacks to begin their humble life in North Dakota. For houses the Germans built a "semeljanka", no doubt a Russian word, made of clay blocks. The blocks were made of clay, straw and water, poured into forms and left for the sun to bake. Fresh clay, water and straw were used as mortar to hold the blocks together and form walls ten to twelve inches thick. Whenever possible flat rock was used for blocks. The roof was made from lumber. These adobes were cool in the summer and warm in the winter. Names like Schwan, Bosch, Schneider, Gefroh, Senger, Vetter, Klein, Keller, Schwab and Lauinger continued to migrate from Russia into Emmons County until about 1914, the time of World War I.

That first group in 1889 broke the prairie and planted flax. This did not yield well, the crop they harvested had to be hauled to Eureka, South Dakota, the nearest railroad and trading center. All the shopping for the following winter was done there, also.

The year 1890 produced another poor crop. The pioneers were getting desperate for meat and flour. They collected buffalo bones and traded them in Napoleon and Steele for flour. Meat was hard to come by since they didn't dare butcher the few stock they had, and the prairie fire had destroyed the wild game.

Fuel for the winter months was a problem since trees were so scarce. Beaver Creek was a rich source of fire wood, many wagon loads were hauled from there.

* * * * *

"MY FIRST WORLD" PEOPLE AND SCHOOL

The citizens in Linton were a mixture of nationalities and religions. The doctors, high school teachers, pharmacist, dentist, lawyers, cattle buyers and other business people came there from various parts of the country.

In contrast, the citizens in Strasburg were mostly Germans from Russia. Seldom was there any language other than German spoken in Strasburg. I always sensed a certain amount of distrust from my father for people who spoke English and were not of his culture. He and his ancestors had been abused by people in Russia. He was cautious when dealing with some of the Linton business people, perhaps these were totally unfounded worries. In Strasburg, business people were "more like one of us" type people.

There was a community of Dutch from Holland in Westfield, near Strasburg whose religion was Dutch Reformed. These Hollanders were proud, education-minded people.

Their well-cared-for farms had beautiful buildings. They appreciated the excellent teachers which the Catholic schools had. The Reformed Church was established in 1916. Mr. M. Van Soest, Sr. offered his home for the first organizational meeting. A church was built in 1917. Reverends B.D. Hietbrink and Ralph Bielema served as pastors in the 1930's. Names such as Van Soest, Borr, Hoogenbuk, Kamp, Niewsma, Pool, Peterman, Haak, Doe and Bole appear in the early history of the church.

Strasburg Public School closed in 1913 when a Catholic school was built. In 1931, finances forced the Catholic school to close. The nun and priest teachers were then hired by the state as teachers and the school continued to operate as a "very special school". This special school status occurred in other parts of North Dakota as well. In 1947 friction over this "very special" situation caused an "Anti-Garb" bill to be passed by the North Dakota Legislature which forced the nuns and priests to remove their religious garb while they were in the classroom. This friction was instigated by a very few people in the state, none were from Strasburg.

* * * * *

NEIGHBORS, THISTLE AND ONION

Government seed and feed loans provided for the desperate spring plantings. The thistles and wild onions that grew were the only crops during those four dry years and were harvested and desperately deployed. The very worst job I ever had in my life had to be hauling dry thistles in hay wagons. The person on top of the hay wagon stacking the thistles had his legs wrapped with several pairs of pants to keep them from being stuck by the thorny barbs. Red, bleeding skin was common. Cow's onion breath was so nostril offending that it was almost impossible to be in the barn with them. They were often milked outside in a little cow fence. The milk and cream took on the onion stench so bad that sometimes creameries turned cream away. Ice cream had a new onion flavor.

Despite all of these struggles, these early farmers were miraculously persistent. They prayed and prayed for rain, planted crops every spring, making the best of the situation and survived. The few rains that did come were in vehement cloud bursts with strong winds lasting about five minutes filling all the gullies. I knew of only one farm in "My Seven Square Mile Area" that changed inhabitants. That was the farm nearest mine, once owned by my grandfather, Mike Keller. Three different families occupied this farm in the 1930's. The first family was my uncle, Peter Keller. He and his wife, Magdalena, had five children, Eddie, Alvina, Lorraine, Henry and Harvey. They moved to Hague. The Mike Vetters were the next family with their mother, Mary Ann and their children Wendelin, Mike, Willie, James, Mary Ann, Clarence, Donnie and Loretta. They moved to a town just inside of the Fargo Diocese. Highway 83 was the demarcation for the Catholic Diocese of Bismarck and the Diocese of Fargo. Today, Wendelin is a priest with the Fargo Diocese. My father is his godfather. The third family who lived on my grandfather's farm was the Frank and Helen Jahner family. They were the parents of seven children, Annie, Mike, Mary, Christine, Marcella, Anton and Pius. The Jahner's moved to Yakima, Washington to work in the apple orchards. Mike was my playmate. He later had the misfortune to die while serving his country during World War II.

The farm just south of mine was that of young Peter Kraft and his wife, Agnes.

Their children were Leonard and Lorraine. I saw this farm develop and then disappear. The Kraft's owned land near our farm. One day a house appeared, then a barn along with some horses and cows and then there was a farm. They were very friendly people. I played often with Leonard. About five years later, the Kraft's moved away. The house and barn were moved away. The circle was completed. At my age then, I just thought that farms always were. I had never given a thought to how they were formed or discontinued.

Even with these bad years the pioneers in "My First World" enjoyed better freedoms and assurances than they had in Russia. Education for their children, freedom to vote and to belong to Farmer's Union organizations pointed to future opportunities. They knew that America was founded on the principle of individual rights, that the state could never take this land or ever use force to coerce them. They knew that hard work would pay off in America.   * * * * *

BOOK REVIEW

"*My First World*" is a genuine slice of North Dakota history.

Sue Neft of the *Williston Herald Daily* wrote this review of *"My First World"*. I would like to share it with you.

By Sue Neft
Williston Herald Daily

"My First World" was written by Dr. Edward Keller, D.D.S. of Dickinson. Because his father was illiterate, and he grew up seeing his father struggle because of this, an education is of prime importance to him.

With the help of Father Charles Meyer, Keller was able to attend high school and college at a seminary in Ohio. He went on to serve as a dental technician for three years in the Army Medical Corps and graduate from St. Thomas College and Dental School. He then moved to Dickinson, where he opened a private dental practice, which he still has.

Keller is presently a journalism student at the University of Dickinson in keeping with his pledge to "never, ever stop learning."

The book is his way of preserving his memories of and love for the seven-mile area enclosed by Strasburg, Linton, the Wells School No. 18, the Rosenthal parish church and the 28 families who lived, worked and worshiped in that area during the first 14 years of his life.

A historical outline of the migration of these "Germans from Russia" is provided in two detailed maps showing the area in Germany and Russia his ancestors migrated from and a third shows, through Keller's own research, where each family homesteaded. Names of families and locations of farms make the book all the more interesting to people familiar with the area depicted.

"*My First World*" is an interesting window on life in a German Catholic farming community. The spirit of the people in the community is hard-working and friendly. The innovation and use of what nature provides is honorable. The long-reaching effects of their faith is obvious.

The memories of a childhood spent close to nature and in loving surroundings are priceless. We would love to provide such a childhood for our children now.

Details of the Depression years are realistic and painful. These are especially interesting for me to put with my own German grandfather's memories for a more complete idea of what the Depression was like on a farm in North Dakota.

The celebrations, for instance of a saint name day, complete with an accordion player sitting in a chair on the dining room table, with the rest of the house converted to a dance floor, makes the reader feel good.

The eulogy of the author to his older sister, Wilma, brought tears for me. Her life, lived out completely in the area described in the book, is a perfect example of the adage "Bloom where you are planted."

Even two delicious memory-invoking recipes are included.

If a book can make you laugh and make you cry, and feel good in between, what more could you ask?

"My First World" by Dr. Edward F. Keller, D.D.S. is available at Books on Broadway in Williston, Linton Drug, *Emmons County Record* and Wagner Super Valu, all of Linton, Pioneer Heritage, Strasburg and by contacting Dr. Keller.